Michael Stonebraker

The Unfiltered Pioneer of Databases – Unauthorized

Liu Yusuf

ISBN: 9781779699848
Imprint: Telephasic Workshop
Copyright © 2024 Liu Yusuf.
All Rights Reserved.

Contents

Introduction   **1**
The Rise of Michael Stonebraker   1

A Legacy Begins   **11**
The Berkeley Years   11

The Stonebraker Database Wars   **33**
Creating Success with Illustra   33

Ups and Downs   **53**
Entrepreneurial Ventures   53
The Academia Journey   70

The Future Awaits   **89**
New Ventures and Innovations   89
The Legacy and Impact   110

Index   **123**

Introduction

The Rise of Michael Stonebraker

Early Beginnings in Computer Science

Michael Stonebraker's journey into the realm of computer science began in an era when the field was still in its infancy. Born in the 1940s, he grew up during a time when the first electronic computers were being developed, laying the groundwork for what would become a revolutionary domain. His early experiences were marked by a curiosity that would later fuel his groundbreaking work in databases.

Stonebraker enrolled at the Massachusetts Institute of Technology (MIT) in the 1960s, a period characterized by rapid advancements in technology and a burgeoning interest in computing. At MIT, he was exposed to the cutting-edge research that would shape his understanding of computer science. The curriculum emphasized a hands-on approach, allowing students to engage with the latest technologies and methodologies. This environment fostered a spirit of innovation and experimentation, which would become hallmarks of Stonebraker's career.

One of the pivotal moments during his academic tenure was his encounter with the concept of data management. At MIT, he was introduced to the early models of database systems, which were primarily hierarchical and network-based. These models, while groundbreaking for their time, presented inherent limitations. For instance, hierarchical databases required a rigid structure that made them inflexible and difficult to manage. This inflexibility often led to data redundancy and integrity issues, which became a significant problem as organizations began to accumulate vast amounts of information.

To illustrate these challenges, consider a simple hierarchical database model representing a university's organizational structure. In this model, each department is linked to a single parent node, creating a tree-like structure. While this model might work for small datasets, it quickly becomes unwieldy as the organization grows. For example, if a new program is introduced that spans multiple departments, the hierarchical structure would require extensive reorganization, leading to potential data loss or inconsistency.

Recognizing these limitations, Stonebraker became increasingly interested in finding solutions that would allow for more flexibility and efficiency in data management. His early work focused on the development of relational database systems, which were emerging as a more robust alternative. The relational model, proposed by Edgar F. Codd in 1970, introduced the concept of organizing data into tables (or relations) that could be easily manipulated using structured query language (SQL). This model allowed for greater flexibility, as data could be accessed and modified without the need for extensive reorganization.

Stonebraker's passion for database systems was further ignited during his time at the University of California, Berkeley, where he began to explore the potential of relational databases. He quickly recognized that the relational model could address many of the challenges posed by hierarchical and network-based systems. The ability to perform complex queries and join multiple tables opened up new avenues for data analysis and management, making it an attractive option for organizations of all sizes.

In 1973, Stonebraker, along with a group of fellow researchers, embarked on a project that would ultimately lead to the creation of Ingres, one of the first relational database management systems (RDBMS). The name Ingres was derived from "Interactive Graphics and Retrieval System," reflecting the system's focus on user interaction and data retrieval capabilities. The development of Ingres marked a significant milestone in Stonebraker's career, as it demonstrated the practical applications of the relational model in real-world scenarios.

The creation of Ingres was not without its challenges. The team faced numerous technical hurdles, including the need to optimize query performance and ensure data integrity. To tackle these issues, Stonebraker and his colleagues implemented innovative algorithms and data structures that would become foundational to the success of Ingres. For example, they developed a sophisticated query optimizer that could efficiently determine the best way to execute a given query, significantly improving performance compared to existing systems.

The impact of Ingres was profound, as it not only provided a viable alternative to hierarchical and network databases but also laid the groundwork for future advancements in database technology. Organizations began to adopt Ingres for its ease of use and flexibility, leading to a shift in the industry towards relational database systems. Stonebraker's early experiences in computer science, coupled with his determination to challenge the status quo, set the stage for a career that would redefine the landscape of data management.

In conclusion, Michael Stonebraker's early beginnings in computer science were characterized by a relentless pursuit of knowledge and a desire to innovate. His academic experiences at MIT and Berkeley provided him with the foundation necessary to tackle the challenges of data management head-on. By embracing the relational model and developing Ingres, Stonebraker not only addressed the limitations of earlier database systems but also paved the way for a new era in data management. His contributions during these formative years would ultimately shape the future of databases and inspire generations of computer scientists to come.

The Unconventional Path to Success

Michael Stonebraker's journey to becoming a luminary in the world of databases was anything but traditional. Born in the mid-1940s, Stonebraker's early years were marked by a profound curiosity and a penchant for challenging the status quo. Rather than following a linear trajectory through academia, he embraced a series of unconventional choices that would ultimately lead him to revolutionize the field of database management systems.

Early Academic Experiences

Stonebraker's academic path began at the Massachusetts Institute of Technology (MIT), where he initially enrolled in the Electrical Engineering program. However, it was during his time at MIT that he discovered his passion for computer science. The burgeoning field of computers was ripe for exploration, and Stonebraker's inquisitive nature propelled him into the world of programming and data management.

His decision to pivot from electrical engineering to computer science was emblematic of his unconventional approach. While many of his peers adhered to prescribed academic routes, Stonebraker sought out opportunities that aligned with his interests, even if they diverged from traditional expectations. This early willingness to explore the unknown would become a hallmark of his career.

The Influence of Rebellion

Stonebraker's journey was also characterized by a sense of rebellion against established norms. In the 1970s, when most database systems were rigid and hierarchical, he recognized the limitations of existing technologies. The prevailing wisdom dictated that databases should be structured in a way that prioritized data integrity over flexibility. However, Stonebraker believed that users should have the freedom to manipulate data in ways that suited their needs.

This philosophy culminated in the development of Ingres, a groundbreaking relational database management system (RDBMS) that challenged the status quo. Ingres was not merely an academic exercise; it was a bold statement that databases could be both powerful and user-friendly. By prioritizing usability, Stonebraker attracted a following of developers and researchers who shared his vision of a more accessible approach to data management.

Embracing Failure as a Stepping Stone

An essential aspect of Stonebraker's unconventional path was his willingness to embrace failure. The road to success is often paved with setbacks, and Stonebraker's journey was no exception. His initial attempts to commercialize Ingres faced significant challenges, including competition from established giants like IBM and Oracle. Rather than succumbing to these obstacles, he viewed them as opportunities for growth.

For instance, the early versions of Ingres encountered performance issues that threatened its viability. Instead of shying away from these problems, Stonebraker and his team tackled them head-on, iterating on their design and refining their approach. This resilience not only improved Ingres but also instilled a culture of innovation within his teams, fostering an environment where experimentation was encouraged.

The Role of Collaboration

Another key element of Stonebraker's unconventional path was his emphasis on collaboration. Throughout his career, he recognized that innovation rarely occurs in isolation. His work at the University of California, Berkeley, was marked by a collaborative spirit that brought together researchers, students, and industry professionals. This environment of shared ideas and collective problem-solving led to the creation of transformative technologies.

Stonebraker's collaboration with fellow researchers resulted in the development of Postgres, an advanced database system that built upon the principles established by Ingres. Postgres introduced features such as support for complex data types and extensibility, further pushing the boundaries of what databases could achieve. The collaborative nature of this work exemplified Stonebraker's belief that the best solutions often arise from diverse perspectives.

Lessons from an Unconventional Path

The unconventional path taken by Michael Stonebraker serves as a testament to the power of curiosity, rebellion, and collaboration in achieving success. His journey underscores several key lessons for aspiring innovators:

- **Follow Your Passion:** Stonebraker's willingness to pivot from electrical engineering to computer science highlights the importance of pursuing what truly interests you, even if it means deviating from conventional paths.
- **Embrace Failure:** Rather than fearing failure, view it as an opportunity for growth. Each setback can provide valuable insights that pave the way for future success.
- **Collaborate and Innovate:** Surround yourself with diverse thinkers and foster an environment of collaboration. The best ideas often emerge from collective brainstorming and shared experiences.

In conclusion, Michael Stonebraker's unconventional path to success is a rich tapestry woven with curiosity, rebellion, and collaboration. His journey serves as an inspiration for those who dare to challenge the norms and redefine the boundaries of what is possible in the world of technology. As we delve deeper into his legacy, it becomes clear that the road less traveled can lead to extraordinary innovations that shape the future.

Embracing Rebellion in the World of Databases

In the realm of computer science, where conformity often reigns supreme, Michael Stonebraker emerged as a beacon of rebellion. His journey through the world of databases is marked by an unwavering commitment to challenge established norms and innovate beyond the accepted boundaries. This section delves into the rebellious spirit that defined Stonebraker's career, exploring the theoretical underpinnings of his approach, the problems he sought to address, and the groundbreaking examples that illustrate his impact.

Theoretical Foundations of Rebellion

At the core of Stonebraker's philosophy lies a fundamental belief that existing database systems were inadequate for the burgeoning needs of data management. Traditional relational databases, while revolutionary in their inception, began to show cracks as data volumes exploded and the complexity of queries increased.

Stonebraker recognized that the rigid structures of these systems could not accommodate the fluidity required by modern applications.

The theoretical framework that guided Stonebraker's rebellion can be traced back to key concepts in database theory, such as normalization, ACID properties, and the relational model itself. While these principles provided a solid foundation for data integrity and consistency, they also imposed constraints that stifled innovation. Stonebraker's insight was to embrace a more flexible approach, one that prioritized performance and adaptability over strict adherence to traditional paradigms.

Identifying Problems in Existing Systems

Stonebraker's rebellious spirit was ignited by the limitations he observed in contemporary database systems. For instance, as organizations began to generate vast amounts of unstructured data—from social media interactions to sensor readings—the need for systems that could efficiently process and analyze this data became paramount. Traditional relational databases struggled to accommodate such diverse data types, often leading to performance bottlenecks and excessive complexity in query formulation.

Moreover, the rise of distributed computing introduced new challenges that legacy systems were ill-equipped to handle. The need for horizontal scalability—the ability to add more machines to handle increased load—was becoming critical. Stonebraker recognized that the monolithic architecture of traditional databases was a significant barrier to achieving this scalability, prompting his quest for alternative solutions.

Stonebraker's Rebellious Innovations

Ingres: A Catalyst for Change Stonebraker's first major act of rebellion came with the creation of Ingres at the University of California, Berkeley. Ingres was not merely an alternative to existing systems; it was a radical rethinking of how databases could operate. By introducing concepts such as query optimization and the use of a relational algebra, Stonebraker challenged the status quo.

The architecture of Ingres allowed for more efficient data retrieval and manipulation. It employed a novel approach to query processing, which involved breaking down complex queries into simpler components that could be executed more efficiently. This was a significant departure from the existing systems that often treated queries as monolithic entities.

$$Q = \text{SELECT } A \text{ FROM } B \text{ WHERE } C \qquad (1)$$

In this equation, Q represents the query, while A, B, and C denote the attributes, tables, and conditions, respectively. Stonebraker's optimization techniques enabled the system to evaluate Q in a more efficient manner, thereby improving performance significantly.

Postgres: The Next Frontier Following the success of Ingres, Stonebraker continued his rebellious journey with the development of Postgres. This system took the principles of Ingres further, introducing support for complex data types and extensibility, which allowed users to define their own data types and functions.

The architecture of Postgres was designed to embrace the evolving landscape of data management. It incorporated a rule-based system for query rewriting, which enabled the database to optimize queries dynamically based on the current workload. This adaptability was revolutionary, as it allowed Postgres to perform better under varying conditions, a feature that traditional systems lacked.

$$R = \text{REWRITE}(Q) \qquad (2)$$

Here, R represents the rewritten query, and the function REWRITE illustrates how Postgres could transform a complex query into a more efficient version, thereby enhancing execution speed and resource utilization.

Illustra and Beyond: Pioneering New Paradigms Stonebraker's rebellion did not stop with Ingres and Postgres; he continued to push boundaries with the creation of Illustra, which introduced object-relational database concepts. This innovation was a direct challenge to the purely relational models, allowing for the storage and retrieval of complex data types, such as images and multimedia, alongside traditional data.

The introduction of column-store databases, exemplified by Mondrian, further illustrated Stonebraker's commitment to redefining data management. By organizing data in columns rather than rows, Mondrian achieved significant performance improvements for analytical queries. This approach not only optimized storage but also accelerated read operations, a critical factor in the age of big data.

Conclusion: The Legacy of Rebellion

Michael Stonebraker's journey through the world of databases is a testament to the power of rebellion in driving innovation. His willingness to challenge established norms and embrace new ideas has profoundly influenced the landscape of data management. Through Ingres, Postgres, Illustra, and Mondrian, Stonebraker has left an indelible mark on the industry, inspiring generations of database professionals to think outside the box.

As we look to the future, the spirit of rebellion that Stonebraker embodies serves as a reminder that true innovation often arises from questioning the status quo. The challenges of tomorrow's data landscape will require thinkers who are unafraid to disrupt conventions and explore uncharted territories in the quest for better solutions. In this sense, Stonebraker's legacy is not merely about the databases he created but about the mindset he fostered—a mindset that continues to inspire and empower the next generation of database pioneers.

The Birth of a Visionary

Michael Stonebraker's journey into the realm of database innovation can be characterized as a confluence of intellect, curiosity, and a rebellious spirit. Born in the post-war era, when computers were still in their infancy, Stonebraker's early fascination with technology set the stage for a career that would redefine how data is stored, accessed, and utilized.

Inception of Ideas

From his formative years at the Massachusetts Institute of Technology (MIT), where he pursued his PhD in Electrical Engineering and Computer Science, Stonebraker was exposed to a myriad of computational theories and practices. His academic endeavors were not merely a pursuit of grades; they were a quest for understanding the very fabric of data management. He often questioned the prevailing paradigms, leading him to explore alternatives that would later become the foundation of his groundbreaking innovations.

One of the pivotal moments in his early career was during the development of the Ingres project at the University of California, Berkeley. Here, he encountered the limitations of traditional database systems, which were primarily designed for specific tasks and lacked the flexibility needed for evolving data requirements. This limitation ignited a spark in Stonebraker—a desire to create a more versatile and robust database architecture.

Challenging Conventional Wisdom

Stonebraker's approach was characterized by a willingness to challenge conventional wisdom. While many of his contemporaries adhered to established methodologies, he sought to disrupt the status quo. The prevailing model of database management at the time was hierarchical or network-based systems, which often led to complexities and inefficiencies.

He famously stated:

> "The best way to predict the future is to invent it."

This philosophy became a guiding principle in his work. Stonebraker's vision was not just to improve existing systems but to revolutionize them entirely. He believed that databases should be designed with the end-user in mind, facilitating ease of access, speed, and scalability.

The Visionary Framework

In his quest to create a new framework for databases, Stonebraker introduced several key concepts that would become hallmarks of modern database systems. One such concept was the relational model, which emphasized the use of tables to represent data and relationships. This model allowed for more straightforward data manipulation and retrieval, setting the stage for the development of Ingres.

The relational model can be mathematically represented as:

$$R(A_1, A_2, \ldots, A_n)$$

where R is a relation and $A_1, A_2, \ldots, A_n$ are attributes. This abstraction not only simplified database design but also laid the groundwork for SQL (Structured Query Language), which became the standard for querying relational databases.

Influencing the Future of Databases

The birth of Stonebraker as a visionary was not solely about technical innovation; it was also about understanding the broader implications of database technology. He recognized that as data began to proliferate, the need for efficient storage and retrieval mechanisms would become paramount.

Stonebraker's work on Ingres demonstrated the potential of relational databases to handle complex queries while maintaining performance. His relentless pursuit of excellence led to the introduction of optimization techniques that improved query execution times, making databases more responsive to user demands.

Moreover, Stonebraker's emphasis on open-source principles during the development of Postgres was groundbreaking. He believed that collaboration and transparency would lead to better software, fostering a community of developers who could contribute to and enhance the database ecosystem. This approach not only democratized access to powerful database tools but also accelerated innovation across the industry.

Conclusion: A Visionary's Legacy

The birth of Michael Stonebraker as a visionary was marked by his ability to foresee the future of data management and his determination to challenge the existing paradigms. His work laid the foundation for a new era in database technology, characterized by flexibility, scalability, and user-centric design.

As we explore the subsequent chapters of his life and career, it becomes clear that Stonebraker's vision was not just about creating databases; it was about transforming the way we interact with data itself. His legacy continues to inspire new generations of database professionals and innovators, ensuring that the spirit of inquiry and rebellion he embodied will endure for years to come.

A Legacy Begins

The Berkeley Years

The Revolutionary Ingres

The development of Ingres in the early 1970s marked a watershed moment in the evolution of database systems, fundamentally altering how data was stored, retrieved, and managed. At its core, Ingres, which stands for "Interactive Graphics and Retrieval System," was born out of a need for a more efficient means of handling data than the existing hierarchical and network database models.

The Birth of Ingres

Michael Stonebraker, alongside his colleagues at the University of California, Berkeley, sought to create a relational database management system (RDBMS) that would leverage the principles of relational algebra as proposed by Edgar F. Codd. The innovative use of the relational model allowed users to interact with data through a high-level query language, SQL (Structured Query Language), which was a significant departure from the more cumbersome navigational methods of data access prevalent at the time.

$$R = \{(A_1, A_2, \ldots, A_n) | P(A_1, A_2, \ldots, A_n)\} \tag{3}$$

In this equation, R represents a relation, $A_1, A_2, \ldots, A_n$ are attributes of the relation, and P denotes a predicate that defines the conditions under which tuples are included in the relation. This mathematical foundation allowed for powerful data manipulation and retrieval.

Challenging the Norms of Database Systems

Ingres was revolutionary not only for its relational model but also for its emphasis on data independence, which allowed changes to the database schema without affecting the applications that relied on it. This concept is encapsulated in the two levels of data independence: logical and physical. Logical data independence allows changes to the logical schema without changing the external schema, while physical data independence allows changes to the physical storage without affecting the logical schema.

One of the primary challenges faced during the development of Ingres was ensuring performance while maintaining the flexibility of the relational model. Early relational systems were often criticized for their inefficiency, particularly in terms of query execution speed. To address this, Stonebraker and his team implemented a sophisticated query optimization engine that utilized various strategies to enhance performance. They introduced the concept of query plans, which are representations of the steps needed to execute a query, allowing the system to choose the most efficient execution path.

Ingres vs. the Giants: The Battle Begins

As Ingres gained traction, it found itself in direct competition with established database systems such as IBM's IMS and IDMS. These systems, built on hierarchical and network models, were deeply entrenched in the enterprise landscape. However, the advantages of Ingres—its ease of use, flexibility, and powerful querying capabilities—began to attract attention.

The first major commercial version of Ingres was released in 1981, and it quickly became a favorite among academic institutions and smaller enterprises. Its success can be attributed to its ability to democratize data access; users no longer needed to be database experts to retrieve and manipulate data. Instead, they could leverage SQL, a language that was more intuitive and accessible.

The Impact and Influence of Ingres

The influence of Ingres on the database landscape cannot be overstated. It laid the groundwork for subsequent relational databases, including Oracle and Microsoft SQL Server, which adopted and built upon its principles. The introduction of SQL as a standard query language became a cornerstone of database interaction, leading to its widespread adoption across various platforms.

Moreover, Ingres was instrumental in the shift toward open systems. Its architecture allowed for greater interoperability and integration with different applications, paving the way for the open-source movement in database technology. The legacy of Ingres continues to resonate, as modern databases still incorporate many of the concepts and innovations pioneered by Stonebraker and his team.

In conclusion, Ingres was more than just a database system; it was a revolution that challenged the status quo, introduced new paradigms of data management, and set the stage for the future of databases. Its legacy is a testament to the visionary spirit of Michael Stonebraker and the collaborative efforts of the Berkeley team, who dared to dream of a better way to handle data.

The Creation of Ingres

The inception of Ingres (Interactive Graphics and Retrieval System) marked a pivotal moment in the evolution of database systems. Developed in the early 1970s at the University of California, Berkeley, Ingres emerged from a desire to create a more efficient, user-friendly database management system that could handle the increasing complexity of data storage and retrieval. Michael Stonebraker, alongside a team of visionary researchers, set out to challenge the existing paradigms of database technology.

Theoretical Foundations

At the heart of Ingres was the relational model proposed by Edgar F. Codd in 1970, which revolutionized how data was structured and accessed. Codd's model emphasized the use of tables (relations) to represent data, allowing for more straightforward data manipulation through a declarative query language. The primary components of the relational model include:

- **Relations:** Data is organized into tables, each consisting of rows and columns.
- **Attributes:** Each column in a table represents a specific attribute of the data.
- **Tuples:** Each row in a table represents a single record or instance of the data.
- **Keys:** Unique identifiers for records, typically primary keys, which ensure that each tuple can be uniquely identified.

The relational algebra, a formal system for manipulating relations, provided the theoretical underpinning for querying data. The key operations include:

$$\text{Select } (\sigma) : \text{Extracts a subset of tuples based on a specified condition.} \quad (4)$$

Project (π) : Retrieves specific attributes from a relation.   (5)

Join (⋈) : Combines tuples from two relations based on a related attribute.   (6)

These operations formed the basis for the Structured Query Language (SQL), which would become the standard for interacting with relational databases.

Design Challenges

Creating Ingres was not without its challenges. One of the primary problems faced by the development team was ensuring that the system could efficiently handle large datasets while maintaining quick response times. Early database systems often struggled with performance issues, particularly as data volumes increased. Stonebraker and his colleagues focused on optimizing query execution and data storage.

A significant innovation was the introduction of query optimization techniques. The Ingres query optimizer analyzed SQL queries to determine the most efficient execution plan. For instance, consider the SQL query:

```
SELECT name, age FROM students WHERE grade = 'A';
```

The optimizer would evaluate various strategies, such as using indexes or performing joins, to minimize the time taken to retrieve the desired data. This optimization was crucial for improving the overall performance of the database.

Key Features of Ingres

Ingres was designed with several groundbreaking features that set it apart from its contemporaries:

- **User-Friendly Interface:** Ingres provided an interactive interface, allowing users to issue queries and receive immediate feedback, which was revolutionary at the time.

- **Data Integrity:** The system implemented constraints to ensure data accuracy and consistency, including primary key constraints and foreign key relationships.

- **Support for Transactions:** Ingres introduced the concept of transactions, allowing multiple operations to be executed as a single unit of work. This was crucial for maintaining data integrity in concurrent environments.

- **Extensibility:** The architecture of Ingres was designed to be modular, enabling future enhancements and the addition of new features without disrupting existing functionality.

Impact and Influence

The release of Ingres had a profound impact on the database landscape. It not only demonstrated the viability of the relational model but also set the stage for the widespread adoption of SQL as the standard language for database management. Ingres inspired a generation of database systems, influencing the development of subsequent products like Oracle and Microsoft SQL Server.

Moreover, Ingres played a significant role in the academic community, serving as a platform for research and experimentation in database technology. The Berkeley team published numerous papers detailing their findings, contributing to the foundational knowledge of database systems.

In conclusion, the creation of Ingres was a landmark achievement that transformed the field of database management. Michael Stonebraker's vision and the collaborative efforts of the Berkeley team led to the development of a system that not only addressed the challenges of data management but also paved the way for future innovations in the industry. The legacy of Ingres continues to resonate, as its principles and concepts remain integral to modern database systems.

Challenging the Norms of Database Systems

In the world of databases, tradition often dictates the rules of engagement. However, Michael Stonebraker, with his audacious spirit and innovative mindset, emerged as a formidable challenger to these established norms. This section explores how Stonebraker's work not only questioned the status quo but also paved the way for revolutionary advancements in database technology.

The Rigid Foundations of Traditional Database Systems

Traditional database systems, primarily based on the relational model proposed by Edgar F. Codd in the 1970s, have long been characterized by their adherence to strict schemas and normalization principles. The relational model emphasizes data integrity and consistency through the use of structured query language (SQL) and normalization techniques. However, these rigid foundations often lead to several inherent problems:

- **Performance Bottlenecks:** As data volumes grew exponentially, traditional systems struggled to maintain performance. The overhead introduced by maintaining strict consistency and integrity checks often resulted in significant latency.

- **Scalability Issues:** The monolithic architecture of traditional databases made horizontal scaling a daunting challenge. Adding more servers often required complex sharding strategies, which could introduce inconsistencies and complicate data management.

- **Inflexibility:** The rigid schema requirements of relational databases limited their ability to adapt to changing data models, which is increasingly critical in the fast-paced world of technology.

Stonebraker's Vision: Redefining Database Architecture

Stonebraker's pioneering work began at the University of California, Berkeley, where he sought to address these limitations. His vision was clear: to create database systems that were not only efficient but also flexible and capable of handling the evolving demands of modern applications. This vision materialized through two groundbreaking projects: Ingres and Postgres.

Ingres: A Step Towards Flexibility Ingres, developed in the late 1970s, was one of the first systems to challenge the rigid structure of traditional databases. It introduced several innovative features:

- **Query Optimization:** Ingres implemented sophisticated query optimization techniques, allowing for faster data retrieval. The introduction of cost-based optimization marked a significant departure from the traditional rule-based approaches.

- **Support for Complex Data Types:** Unlike its predecessors, Ingres allowed users to define new data types, thereby enhancing the system's adaptability to various applications.

The success of Ingres demonstrated that it was possible to maintain data integrity while also providing the flexibility needed for modern applications.

Postgres: The Next Evolution Building on the lessons learned from Ingres, Stonebraker spearheaded the development of Postgres in the mid-1980s. Postgres sought to address the limitations of traditional relational databases even further by introducing several key innovations:

- **Object-Relational Features:** Postgres integrated object-oriented concepts into the relational model, allowing for the storage of complex data types and relationships. This shift enabled developers to model real-world entities more accurately.

- **Extensibility:** Postgres was designed with extensibility in mind, allowing users to create custom data types, operators, and functions. This feature empowered developers to tailor the database to their specific needs without compromising performance.

- **MVCC (Multi-Version Concurrency Control):** Postgres adopted MVCC to handle concurrent transactions more efficiently. This approach minimized locking issues, allowing for greater throughput and improved performance in multi-user environments.

Challenging the Status Quo: The Impact of Stonebraker's Work

Stonebraker's relentless pursuit of innovation did not go unnoticed. His work laid the groundwork for a series of paradigm shifts in the database industry. The impact of his contributions can be summarized as follows:

- **Inspiring Future Innovations:** The concepts introduced by Stonebraker have inspired a new generation of database systems, including NoSQL databases, which prioritize flexibility and scalability over strict adherence to relational principles.

- **Shaping Industry Standards:** The features pioneered by Ingres and Postgres have become foundational elements in modern database systems, influencing the design of many subsequent technologies.

- **Encouraging a Culture of Experimentation:** Stonebraker's willingness to challenge norms encouraged other researchers and developers to explore new ideas and approaches in database design, fostering a culture of innovation in the field.

Conclusion

Michael Stonebraker's journey through the world of databases is a testament to the power of challenging established norms. By questioning the rigidity of traditional systems and advocating for flexibility and innovation, he not only transformed the landscape of database technology but also inspired countless others to push the boundaries of what is possible. His legacy serves as a reminder that true progress often requires a willingness to defy convention and embrace the unknown.

Ingres vs. the Giants: The Battle Begins

The advent of Ingres marked a pivotal moment in the history of database management systems (DBMS). As Michael Stonebraker and his team at the University of California, Berkeley, embarked on this ambitious project, they found themselves entering a battleground dominated by established giants such as IBM, Oracle, and Digital Equipment Corporation (DEC). This section delves into the challenges posed by these industry behemoths and how Ingres sought to carve its niche amidst fierce competition.

The Landscape of Database Giants

In the early 1980s, the database industry was characterized by a few dominant players. IBM's DB2 was synonymous with reliability and enterprise-level performance, while Oracle was making waves with its innovative approach to relational databases. DEC's Rdb was also a significant contender, boasting a strong presence in the minicomputer market. These giants had robust financial backing, extensive marketing resources, and established customer bases, making it daunting for newcomers like Ingres to gain traction.

Identifying the Gaps

Stonebraker and his team recognized that to succeed, they needed to identify gaps in the offerings of these giants. They focused on several key areas:

- **Cost-Effectiveness:** The licensing fees and hardware requirements of the giants often placed their products out of reach for smaller companies and academic institutions. Ingres aimed to provide a more affordable alternative without compromising on performance.

- **User-Friendly Interfaces:** Many existing systems were notoriously difficult to use. Ingres sought to develop a more intuitive interface that catered to the needs of users who were not database experts.

- **Flexibility and Extensibility:** The rigidity of existing systems often stifled innovation. Ingres was designed to be modular, allowing users to extend its capabilities easily.

Innovative Features of Ingres

To differentiate itself from the giants, Ingres introduced several groundbreaking features:

- **Query Language:** Ingres utilized a powerful query language based on SQL (Structured Query Language), which allowed users to interact with the database in a more straightforward manner. This was a significant departure from the more complex query languages used by competitors.

- **Transaction Management:** Ingres implemented robust transaction management features, ensuring data integrity and consistency. This was particularly important in multi-user environments where concurrent access to data was common.

- **Support for Complex Data Types:** Unlike many of its competitors, Ingres allowed for the storage and manipulation of complex data types, catering to a wider range of applications.

The Battle for Market Share

As Ingres began to gain traction, the giants responded with a mix of skepticism and aggression. IBM and Oracle launched aggressive marketing campaigns to reinforce their market dominance, often downplaying the capabilities of Ingres. However, the growing interest from academic institutions and smaller enterprises began to shift the narrative.

Real-World Applications: The Ingres Advantage

One of the most compelling aspects of Ingres was its application in real-world scenarios. For instance, the University of California, Berkeley, utilized Ingres for various research projects, demonstrating its effectiveness in handling large datasets.

This not only validated the technology but also showcased its potential to a broader audience.

$$\text{Performance}_{Ingres} = \frac{\text{Throughput} \times \text{Response Time}}{\text{Cost}} \qquad (7)$$

The equation above illustrates the core performance metrics that Ingres aimed to optimize. By maximizing throughput while minimizing response time and cost, Ingres positioned itself as a viable alternative to the giants.

The Turning Point

The turning point for Ingres came when it was adopted by several high-profile organizations, including government agencies and research institutions. Their success stories served as testimonials to the capabilities of Ingres, further solidifying its reputation.

As the battle raged on, Ingres began to establish itself not just as a competitor but as a legitimate player in the database landscape. Its innovative approach and user-centric design resonated with a growing audience, leading to increased adoption and recognition.

Conclusion: The Impact of Ingres

The emergence of Ingres not only challenged the status quo but also forced the giants to reevaluate their strategies. The competitive pressure exerted by Ingres led to innovations across the industry, benefiting users and setting the stage for the future of database technology.

In conclusion, the battle between Ingres and the giants was not merely a struggle for market share; it was a transformative moment that reshaped the landscape of database management systems. Stonebraker's vision and the team's relentless pursuit of excellence laid the groundwork for a new era in database technology, one where innovation and user needs took precedence over established norms.

The Impact and Influence of Ingres

The development of Ingres marked a pivotal moment in the evolution of database management systems (DBMS), fundamentally altering the landscape of data storage and retrieval. As one of the first relational database systems, Ingres was not merely a product of its time but a harbinger of the future, influencing countless systems that followed. This section delves into the profound impact and influence of Ingres

Theoretical Foundations

At the core of Ingres's design was the relational model proposed by Edgar F. Codd in 1970. Codd's model introduced a structured way to manage data using tables, which allowed for more flexible and efficient data manipulation compared to the hierarchical and network models that preceded it. The fundamental principles of the relational model, including data independence, normalization, and the use of Structured Query Language (SQL), were integral to Ingres's architecture.

$$R = \{(a_1, a_2, \ldots, a_n)\} \tag{8}$$

In this equation, R represents a relation (or table) containing tuples (rows) of attributes (columns). The emphasis on set theory and mathematical logic provided a solid foundation for querying and managing data, allowing users to perform complex operations with relative ease.

Practical Applications and Innovations

Ingres was not just an academic exercise; it found practical applications in various domains, from business to research. One of its most significant contributions was the introduction of SQL, which became the standard language for querying relational databases. SQL's declarative nature allowed users to specify what data they wanted without detailing how to retrieve it, significantly lowering the barrier to entry for database management.

$$SELECT\ column_1, column_2\ FROM\ table\ WHERE\ condition; \tag{9}$$

This simple SQL query exemplifies how Ingres democratized data access, enabling users from diverse backgrounds to interact with databases effectively. The widespread adoption of SQL can be traced back to Ingres, which set the stage for its incorporation into various other systems, including Oracle and Microsoft SQL Server.

Performance and Efficiency

Another critical impact of Ingres was its focus on performance and efficiency. The introduction of query optimization techniques allowed Ingres to execute queries faster than its predecessors. The optimizer analyzed different execution plans and selected the most efficient one based on the available indexes and statistics.

For instance, consider a query that retrieves customer records from a large dataset. Without optimization, the system might perform a full table scan, which is computationally expensive. Ingres's optimizer would evaluate possible strategies, such as using an index on the customer ID, thus significantly improving performance.

Influence on Subsequent Database Systems

The influence of Ingres extended far beyond its immediate applications. Its architectural innovations and theoretical contributions laid the groundwork for subsequent relational database systems. Notably, systems like Postgres, which Michael Stonebraker later developed, were heavily inspired by Ingres's design principles. The concept of extensibility and support for complex data types in Postgres can be traced back to the foundational work done with Ingres.

Furthermore, Ingres's emphasis on open-source principles fostered a collaborative environment that encouraged innovation. This spirit of openness paved the way for the development of other open-source database systems, such as MySQL and PostgreSQL, which continue to thrive today.

Legacy and Continuing Relevance

The legacy of Ingres is evident in the continued relevance of its principles in modern database systems. Concepts such as normalization, ACID properties (Atomicity, Consistency, Isolation, Durability), and the use of SQL remain cornerstones of database management today. The relational model's ability to adapt to new requirements, such as distributed databases and cloud computing, further underscores its enduring significance.

Moreover, Ingres's impact can be seen in the evolution of database technologies addressing big data challenges. While traditional relational databases may struggle with unstructured data, the foundational concepts established by Ingres continue to inform the development of hybrid systems that integrate relational and non-relational data models.

Conclusion

In summary, the impact and influence of Ingres on the field of database management systems cannot be overstated. From its theoretical foundations rooted in the relational model to its practical applications and innovations, Ingres set a standard that continues to shape the industry. As we explore the legacy of Michael Stonebraker and his contributions to databases, it is essential to recognize Ingres as a cornerstone of modern data management, a testament to the power of innovation and the relentless pursuit of excellence in the world of technology.

Pioneering Postgres

In the annals of database history, few names resonate as profoundly as that of Postgres, a groundbreaking project that emerged from the innovative mind of Michael Stonebraker and his team at the University of California, Berkeley. Postgres, short for "Post-Ingres," was conceived as a response to the limitations of its predecessor, Ingres, and aimed to address the burgeoning needs of modern database applications in the late 1980s.

The Genesis of Postgres

The journey of Postgres began in 1986, during a time when relational databases were becoming the standard for data management. However, as applications grew increasingly complex, the relational model faced challenges in handling advanced data types and complex queries. Recognizing these limitations, Stonebraker sought to create a system that could not only support traditional relational data but also accommodate new data types, such as object-oriented constructs.

The core philosophy behind Postgres was to extend the relational database model to include features that would allow for more complex data representations. This led to the introduction of the concept of "object-relational" databases, which combined the best of both worlds.

Innovative Features and Theoretical Underpinnings

At the heart of Postgres was the notion of extensibility. Unlike traditional databases that were rigid in their data types, Postgres allowed users to define their own data types and functions. This was achieved through a powerful type system and a sophisticated query language that built upon SQL, incorporating elements from functional programming.

One of the key theoretical contributions of Postgres was the implementation of the **Rule System**. This system allowed users to define rules for how data should be transformed or manipulated during query execution. For example, a rule could be created to automatically update a derived table whenever the underlying data changed, enhancing the efficiency of data management.

The architecture of Postgres was also revolutionary. It employed a **multi-version concurrency control (MVCC)** mechanism, which enabled multiple transactions to occur simultaneously without interfering with one another. This was a significant advancement over traditional locking mechanisms, as it reduced contention and improved performance in high-transaction environments.

$$\text{MVCC}(t) = \frac{\sum_{i=1}^{n}(V_i(t) - L_i(t))}{n}$$

where $V_i(t)$ represents the version of the data at time t, and $L_i(t)$ is the lock state of the data at time t.

Postgres and the Open Source Movement

The release of Postgres as an open-source project in the early 1990s was a watershed moment in its history. By making the source code available to the public, Stonebraker and his team fostered a community of developers who contributed to its evolution. This collaborative spirit not only accelerated the development of Postgres but also ensured its adaptability to a wide range of applications.

The open-source nature of Postgres also allowed it to compete effectively with proprietary database systems, which often required hefty licensing fees and were slow to innovate. As a result, Postgres gained traction among developers and organizations that valued flexibility and cost-effectiveness.

Challenges and Triumphs

Despite its innovative features, Postgres faced significant challenges during its early years. One of the primary hurdles was performance. While the extensibility and advanced features of Postgres were groundbreaking, they came at the cost of speed. Early adopters often reported slower query performance compared to established systems like Oracle and DB2.

To address these issues, the Postgres team focused on optimization techniques, including query rewriting and indexing strategies. The introduction of **B-tree** and **hash indexing** significantly improved data retrieval speeds, allowing Postgres to handle larger datasets more efficiently.

Postgres in the Modern Era

Today, Postgres stands as a testament to the vision of Michael Stonebraker and his pioneering spirit. It has evolved into one of the most robust and widely used database systems globally, powering applications across various industries. The introduction of features such as JSONB support for semi-structured data, full-text search capabilities, and advanced indexing methods has solidified its position as a leader in the database landscape.

Moreover, the rise of cloud computing and the demand for scalable database solutions have further propelled Postgres into the spotlight. With the advent of cloud-based services like Amazon RDS and Google Cloud SQL, organizations can leverage the power of Postgres without the overhead of managing physical infrastructure.

Conclusion

In conclusion, the pioneering efforts behind Postgres not only transformed the landscape of database management but also laid the groundwork for future innovations in the field. Michael Stonebraker's vision of an extensible, object-relational database has proven to be a lasting legacy, inspiring generations of developers and researchers to push the boundaries of what is possible in data management. As we look to the future, the principles established by Postgres will undoubtedly continue to influence the evolution of database technologies for years to come.

The Birth of Postgres: A Database Revolution

The birth of Postgres in the late 1980s marked a pivotal moment in the evolution of database systems, driven by the visionary mind of Michael Stonebraker and his team at the University of California, Berkeley. Postgres, short for "Post-Ingres," was conceived as a response to the limitations of traditional relational database management systems (RDBMS) and aimed to incorporate advanced features that would redefine how data was stored, accessed, and manipulated.

The Vision Behind Postgres

At its core, Postgres was designed to extend the capabilities of its predecessor, Ingres, by integrating object-oriented concepts into the relational model. This was a radical shift that sought to address the growing complexity of data and the need for more sophisticated data types. Stonebraker envisioned a system that could handle not just simple data types such as integers and strings, but also complex data structures like arrays, records, and even user-defined types.

One of the foundational theories that guided the development of Postgres was the notion of *extensibility*. This concept allowed users to define their own data types and functions, thus enabling the database to adapt to a wide range of applications. The ability to create custom types and functions is encapsulated in the following equation:

$$D = f(T, F, R) \quad (10)$$

where D represents the database, T is the set of data types, F is the set of functions, and R is the relational model. This equation highlights the interplay between data types, functions, and the relational structure, showcasing how Postgres aimed to provide a more flexible and powerful database environment.

Challenges and Innovations

The development of Postgres was not without its challenges. One of the primary problems faced by the team was ensuring compatibility with existing SQL standards while also pushing the boundaries of what a database could do. The team had to navigate the delicate balance between innovation and usability, ensuring that the new features did not alienate users accustomed to traditional RDBMS.

To tackle this, Stonebraker and his team implemented a rule-based query processor, which allowed for more complex queries and optimizations. This innovation was a significant leap forward from the query processing capabilities of Ingres, enabling users to write more sophisticated queries without sacrificing performance.

An example of this can be seen in the way Postgres handled joins. Traditional RDBMS often struggled with complex joins involving multiple tables, leading to performance bottlenecks. Postgres introduced advanced join algorithms, including hash joins and merge joins, which significantly improved query execution times. The efficiency of these operations can be represented as:

$$T_{join} = \frac{N_1 + N_2}{C} \quad (11)$$

where T_{join} is the time taken to execute the join, N_1 and N_2 are the number of records in the joining tables, and C is the efficiency constant determined by the join algorithm employed. This formula underscored the importance of algorithmic efficiency in database performance.

The Impact of Postgres

The release of Postgres was a watershed moment that reverberated throughout the database industry. Its capabilities set new standards for what a database system could achieve, particularly in the realm of complex data management and extensibility. The system's ability to handle diverse data types and structures made it particularly appealing to developers working in fields such as scientific computing, data analysis, and application development.

Postgres also played a crucial role in the burgeoning open-source movement. By releasing Postgres as an open-source project, Stonebraker and his team democratized access to advanced database technology, allowing developers around the world to contribute to its evolution. This collaborative approach fostered a vibrant community that propelled Postgres to new heights, leading to widespread adoption and continuous improvement.

The significance of Postgres can be summarized in the following equation, which highlights its transformative impact on the database landscape:

$$I = \sum_{i=1}^{n} E_i \qquad (12)$$

where I represents the overall impact of Postgres, and E_i denotes the individual enhancements and innovations introduced by the system. Each enhancement contributed to the collective legacy of Postgres, which continues to influence database design and implementation to this day.

In conclusion, the birth of Postgres was not merely the introduction of another database system; it was a revolution that challenged the status quo, expanded the horizons of data management, and laid the groundwork for future innovations in the field. Michael Stonebraker's vision, combined with the team's dedication to pushing the boundaries of technology, ensured that Postgres would leave an indelible mark on the world of databases, paving the way for a new era of data-driven applications and solutions.

The Significance of Postgres in the Database Landscape

PostgreSQL, affectionately known as Postgres, emerged as a groundbreaking force in the realm of database management systems (DBMS). Its significance in the database landscape can be attributed to several key factors that not only reflect its technological advancements but also its philosophical underpinnings and community-driven ethos.

1. Advanced Features and Extensibility

One of the hallmarks of Postgres is its rich feature set, which includes support for advanced data types, complex queries, and extensible architecture. Unlike many of its contemporaries, Postgres supports a variety of data types, including JSON, XML, and even user-defined types. This flexibility allows developers to model complex data structures that are often required in modern applications.

The ability to define custom data types is particularly noteworthy. For instance, consider a scenario where a developer is creating an application that manages geographical information. By leveraging Postgres's extensibility, the developer can create a custom type for geographic coordinates, enabling more intuitive queries:

```
CREATE TYPE geo_point AS (
    latitude\index{latitude} FLOAT,
    longitude\index{longitude} FLOAT
);
```

This feature not only enhances the database's usability but also empowers developers to create more sophisticated applications tailored to their specific needs.

2. SQL Compliance and Robustness

Postgres is renowned for its adherence to SQL standards, making it a reliable choice for developers who prioritize compliance and consistency. According to the SQL standard, a compliant DBMS should support a wide range of functionalities, including transaction management, data integrity, and concurrency control. Postgres excels in these areas, offering features such as:

- **ACID Compliance:** PostgreSQL ensures that all transactions are Atomic, Consistent, Isolated, and Durable (ACID). This guarantees data integrity even in the face of system failures or concurrent transactions.

- **MVCC:** Multi-Version Concurrency Control (MVCC) allows multiple transactions to occur simultaneously without locking the entire database, thus improving performance and user experience.

The robustness of Postgres makes it particularly suitable for mission-critical applications where data integrity and reliability are paramount.

3. Open Source Community and Innovation

Another significant aspect of Postgres's impact is its open-source nature. The database has a vibrant community of developers and users who contribute to its continuous improvement. This collaborative environment fosters innovation, allowing new features and enhancements to be developed rapidly. For example, the introduction of the Just-in-Time (JIT) compilation feature in PostgreSQL 11 significantly improved query performance, showcasing the community's responsiveness to user needs.

The open-source model also means that organizations can adopt Postgres without the burden of licensing fees, making it an attractive option for startups and enterprises alike. The freedom to modify and distribute the software has led to a diverse ecosystem of tools and extensions that enhance Postgres's capabilities, such as PostGIS for geographic information systems and TimescaleDB for time-series data.

4. Scalability and Performance

Postgres has evolved to meet the demands of modern applications, particularly in terms of scalability and performance. With features like partitioning, parallel query execution, and advanced indexing options, Postgres can handle large datasets and high transaction volumes efficiently. The ability to scale both vertically and horizontally allows organizations to adapt their database infrastructure as their needs grow.

For instance, consider a large e-commerce platform that experiences fluctuating traffic. By utilizing Postgres's partitioning capabilities, the platform can distribute data across multiple partitions, improving query performance and reducing response times during peak usage. This adaptability is a crucial factor in maintaining competitive advantage in today's fast-paced digital landscape.

5. Adoption and Industry Impact

Postgres's significance is further underscored by its widespread adoption across various industries. Major companies like Apple, Cisco, and Instagram rely on Postgres for their database needs, demonstrating its reliability and performance at scale. The database's role in powering applications across sectors such as finance, healthcare, and education highlights its versatility and robustness.

Moreover, Postgres has influenced the development of other database systems. Its innovative features and open-source philosophy have inspired many NoSQL databases, which often incorporate similar concepts of flexibility and scalability. The rise of cloud-based database services, such as Amazon RDS for PostgreSQL, has further solidified its position in the market, making it accessible to a broader audience.

Conclusion

In summary, the significance of Postgres in the database landscape is multifaceted. Its advanced features, robust performance, and open-source community have established it as a leading choice for developers and organizations alike. As data continues to grow in complexity and volume, Postgres's adaptability and innovative spirit will undoubtedly ensure its relevance for years to come. The legacy of Postgres is not just in its technology, but in its ability to empower users to harness the full potential of their data, making it a true pioneer in the world of databases.

The Open Source Movement: Changing the Game

The open source movement has fundamentally transformed the landscape of software development, particularly in the realm of databases. At the heart of this revolution is the idea that software should be freely available for use, modification, and distribution. This section explores how Michael Stonebraker's contributions to open source databases have not only changed the game for developers but have also democratized access to powerful database technologies.

The Philosophy of Open Source

Open source software (OSS) is rooted in the philosophy of collaboration and transparency. Unlike proprietary software, where the source code is locked away, OSS allows anyone to inspect, modify, and enhance the code. This approach fosters innovation and community engagement, as developers from diverse backgrounds can contribute their expertise. The Open Source Initiative (OSI) defines open source software as software that grants users the freedom to run, study, change, and distribute the software and its source code.

Stonebraker's Vision for Open Source

Michael Stonebraker was a visionary who recognized the potential of open source databases to disrupt the status quo. His work on Postgres in the late 1980s laid the groundwork for what would become a significant player in the open source database arena. By releasing Postgres under an open source license, Stonebraker enabled a global community of developers to engage with the technology, leading to rapid advancements and a wealth of contributions.

Key Contributions to Open Source Databases

One of Stonebraker's most notable contributions is the PostgreSQL project, which emerged from the Postgres research project at the University of California, Berkeley. PostgreSQL is a powerful, open source object-relational database system that has gained widespread adoption due to its robustness and extensibility. The transition from Postgres to PostgreSQL marked a significant milestone in the open source movement.

The architectural design of PostgreSQL allows for complex queries and supports a wide range of data types, making it suitable for various applications, from simple websites to complex data warehousing solutions. Its strong adherence to SQL standards and continuous development by a dedicated community have made PostgreSQL a cornerstone of modern database management.

The Impact of Open Source on Database Development

The rise of open source databases has shifted the dynamics of the database industry. Companies that once relied solely on proprietary solutions began to recognize the advantages of open source technologies. For instance, organizations could avoid vendor lock-in, reduce licensing costs, and leverage community support for troubleshooting and enhancements.

Furthermore, the open source model has encouraged innovation. Developers can experiment with new features and functionalities without the constraints imposed by proprietary systems. This has led to the emergence of various open source database solutions, each catering to specific use cases. For example, MongoDB, an open source NoSQL database, has gained popularity for handling unstructured data, while MySQL remains a go-to choice for web applications.

Challenges and Criticisms of Open Source Databases

Despite the numerous benefits, the open source movement is not without its challenges. One significant concern is the sustainability of open source projects. Many rely on volunteer contributions, which can lead to inconsistent updates and support. Additionally, the lack of formal support can be daunting for organizations that require guaranteed service levels.

Another criticism of open source databases is security. While the transparency of open source code allows for easier identification of vulnerabilities, it also means that malicious actors can exploit these weaknesses before they are patched. Organizations must adopt robust security practices and stay vigilant to mitigate these risks.

Conclusion: A Lasting Legacy

Michael Stonebraker's pioneering efforts in the open source movement have had a lasting impact on the database industry. By championing open source principles, he has empowered a generation of developers to create innovative solutions that challenge traditional norms. The democratization of database technology has opened doors to new possibilities, enabling organizations of all sizes to harness the power of data without the constraints of proprietary systems.

As we look to the future, the open source movement continues to evolve, driven by the same spirit of collaboration and innovation that Stonebraker embodied. The legacy of open source databases is a testament to the transformative power of community-driven development, and it will undoubtedly shape the future of technology for years to come.

The Stonebraker Database Wars

Creating Success with Illustra

The Evolution of Illustra

The story of Illustra is one of ambition, innovation, and a relentless pursuit of redefining the boundaries of database technology. Founded in the early 1990s, Illustra emerged from the fertile grounds of research and development at the University of California, Berkeley, where Michael Stonebraker and his team sought to address the evolving needs of data management in an increasingly complex digital landscape.

The Genesis of Illustra

Illustra was conceived as a response to the limitations of traditional relational database systems. While these systems had dominated the market, they struggled to manage complex data types such as images, text, and spatial data. The rise of the internet and the explosion of multimedia content necessitated a shift towards more versatile database solutions. Stonebraker recognized this gap and envisioned a system that could handle not only structured data but also semi-structured and unstructured data.

$$D = \{d_1, d_2, \ldots, d_n\} \qquad (13)$$

where D represents the dataset, and each d_i can be of varying types, including structured, semi-structured, and unstructured formats.

Key Features of Illustra

Illustra introduced several revolutionary features that set it apart from its predecessors. One of the most significant innovations was the ability to store and query complex data types directly within the database. This was achieved through the implementation of object-relational database management systems (ORDBMS), which combined the best of both relational and object-oriented paradigms.

- **User-Defined Types (UDTs):** Illustra allowed users to define their own data types, enabling the storage of complex structures such as images and audio files directly in the database.

- **Advanced Querying Capabilities:** The introduction of new query languages and extensions to SQL facilitated the retrieval and manipulation of complex data types.

- **Multimedia Support:** Illustra was one of the first databases to natively support multimedia data, paving the way for applications in fields such as digital libraries and geographic information systems (GIS).

Challenges and Market Reception

Despite its innovative features, Illustra faced significant challenges in gaining market traction. The database industry was heavily dominated by established players such as Oracle and IBM, which had entrenched customer bases and robust marketing strategies. Illustra's entry into the market was met with skepticism, as many organizations were hesitant to transition from their existing systems.

Moreover, the complexity of implementing an object-relational system posed additional hurdles. Organizations had to invest in retraining their staff and rethinking their data management strategies. This resistance to change was a common theme in the evolution of new technologies, as illustrated by the following equation representing the adoption curve:

$$A(t) = \frac{K}{1 + e^{-r(t-t_0)}} \qquad (14)$$

where $A(t)$ is the adoption rate at time t, K is the maximum potential adoption, r is the growth rate, and t_0 is the inflection point of adoption.

The Impact of Illustra on Database Technology

Despite its challenges, Illustra's impact on the database landscape was profound. It laid the groundwork for future developments in object-relational databases and influenced subsequent database systems. The concepts introduced by Illustra, such as UDTs and advanced querying capabilities, became foundational elements in later database technologies.

The legacy of Illustra can be seen in the evolution of databases that continue to support complex data types and the increasing emphasis on flexibility in data management. Stonebraker's vision of a more versatile database system resonated with the growing demand for handling diverse data formats, ultimately leading to the rise of modern databases that prioritize user-defined data structures.

Conclusion

In conclusion, the evolution of Illustra is a testament to the innovative spirit of Michael Stonebraker and his team. By challenging the status quo and addressing the limitations of existing database systems, Illustra not only carved out its niche in the market but also paved the way for future advancements in database technology. The lessons learned from Illustra's journey continue to inform the development of new database solutions, ensuring that the legacy of this pioneering system endures in the ever-evolving world of data management.

From Concept to Reality: The Journey of Illustra

The story of Illustra is not merely one of technological advancement; it is a saga of vision, perseverance, and the relentless pursuit of innovation in the realm of databases. Founded in the early 1990s, Illustra emerged from a confluence of ideas that sought to address the growing complexity of data management, particularly in relation to multimedia data types. This section will delve into the evolution of Illustra, highlighting key theoretical foundations, challenges faced during development, and the transformative impact it had on the database landscape.

Theoretical Foundations

At its core, Illustra was built upon the principles of object-relational database management systems (ORDBMS). Unlike traditional relational databases, which primarily focused on structured data, Illustra aimed to integrate complex data types, including text, images, and video, into a unified framework. This shift was grounded in the need for a more flexible approach to data storage and retrieval, reflecting the diverse nature of modern applications.

The theoretical underpinnings of Illustra can be traced back to the work of Michael Stonebraker and his colleagues at the University of California, Berkeley. They recognized that conventional relational models, while powerful, were ill-equipped to handle the burgeoning demands of multimedia data. This realization led to the conceptualization of a system that would extend the relational model by incorporating object-oriented principles.

The foundational equation that guided the design of Illustra can be expressed as:

$$D = R \cup C \qquad (15)$$

where D represents the data model of Illustra, R denotes the relational component, and C signifies the complex data types. This equation encapsulates the hybrid nature of Illustra, bridging the gap between traditional relational databases and the emerging need for complex data handling.

Development Challenges

The journey from concept to reality was fraught with challenges. One of the primary hurdles was the integration of complex data types into the existing relational framework. Developers faced numerous technical obstacles, including the need for new indexing techniques that could efficiently handle non-standard data types.

For instance, the introduction of a new indexing mechanism, known as the *Multimedia Index*, was crucial for optimizing the retrieval of image and video data. This index utilized a combination of spatial and temporal dimensions to enhance query performance, a significant departure from traditional B-tree indexing methods.

The development team also grappled with performance issues. Early prototypes of Illustra struggled with scalability, particularly when handling large volumes of multimedia data. To address this, the team implemented advanced caching strategies and optimized query processing algorithms, which significantly improved the system's responsiveness.

Real-World Applications

As Illustra transitioned from a conceptual framework to a fully-fledged product, its applications began to emerge in various industries. One notable example was in the field of digital libraries, where the ability to manage and retrieve multimedia content became increasingly vital. Illustra's architecture allowed institutions to store vast collections of images, videos, and texts, making it an invaluable tool for research and education.

Moreover, the healthcare industry recognized the potential of Illustra for managing complex patient data, including medical images, electronic health records, and genomic data. The ability to query and analyze this multifaceted information in a unified manner provided healthcare professionals with deeper insights and improved patient outcomes.

The impact of Illustra was not limited to specific sectors; it also influenced the broader database landscape. Its introduction of object-relational features prompted other database vendors to explore similar innovations, effectively shifting the paradigm of data management.

Conclusion

The journey of Illustra from concept to reality exemplifies the spirit of innovation that defines Michael Stonebraker's career. By challenging conventional wisdom and embracing the complexities of modern data, Illustra set a new standard for database systems. Its legacy continues to resonate in the ongoing evolution of database technology, reminding us that the quest for knowledge and understanding is an ever-evolving journey.

In summary, Illustra's development was marked by theoretical advancements, technical challenges, and real-world applications that collectively transformed the database landscape. As we move forward, it is essential to recognize the significance of such pioneering efforts in shaping the future of data management.

Revolutionary Features of Illustra: Redefining Databases

In the ever-evolving landscape of database technology, Illustra emerged as a groundbreaking player that redefined the very essence of how databases were perceived and utilized. Launched in the early 1990s, Illustra was not merely another database management system; it was a harbinger of innovation that introduced several revolutionary features which would go on to influence the design and functionality of modern databases.

Object-Relational Database Management System (ORDBMS)

At the core of Illustra's innovation was its classification as an Object-Relational Database Management System (ORDBMS). This was a significant departure from the traditional relational database systems that dominated the market. The fundamental premise behind ORDBMS was to integrate the principles of object-oriented programming with the relational model.

The object-relational model allowed for the storage of complex data types, enabling users to define custom data types, or objects, that could encapsulate both data and behavior. For instance, consider a scenario in a university database where a 'Student' object could not only store attributes like 'name', 'ID', and 'courses', but also include methods to calculate GPA or check enrollment status. This encapsulation facilitated more intuitive data manipulation and retrieval.

$$\text{GPA} = \frac{\sum_{i=1}^{n}(\text{Grade}_i \times \text{Credits}_i)}{\sum_{i=1}^{n}\text{Credits}_i} \qquad (16)$$

This equation illustrates how GPA can be calculated using the grades and credits associated with each course, emphasizing the integration of behavior (method) with data (object).

Support for Complex Data Types

Illustra's support for complex data types was another revolutionary feature. Traditional relational databases were limited to scalar data types such as integers, strings, and floats. However, Illustra allowed users to define and utilize more sophisticated data structures, such as arrays, multimedia data types (like images and audio), and even user-defined types.

For example, a 'Video' data type could be created to store not just the file path to a video but also metadata such as duration, resolution, and format. This capability was particularly beneficial for applications in fields like multimedia, scientific research, and geographical information systems (GIS), where the need to manage complex data sets was paramount.

Advanced Query Language: SQL3

To complement its object-relational capabilities, Illustra introduced an advanced query language known as SQL3, which extended the SQL standard with object-oriented features. This language allowed developers to perform complex queries that could navigate through the intricate relationships between objects.

For instance, a query to retrieve all students enrolled in a specific course, along with their GPAs, could be expressed in SQL3 as follows:

```
SELECT Student.name, Student.calculateGPA()
```

```
FROM Student
JOIN Enrollment ON Student.ID = Enrollment.StudentID
WHERE Enrollment.CourseID = 'CS101';
```

This query not only retrieves the names of students but also invokes the method to calculate their GPAs, showcasing the seamless integration of data and behavior.

Multidimensional Data Support

Illustra also pioneered support for multidimensional data, which was particularly useful for applications that required analysis across multiple dimensions, such as data warehousing and business intelligence. This feature allowed users to perform complex analytical queries on data organized in a multidimensional structure, often referred to as "cubes."

The concept of a data cube can be represented mathematically as:

$$\text{Cube}(X, Y, Z) = \{(x, y, z) \mid x \in X, y \in Y, z \in Z\} \tag{17}$$

Where X, Y, and Z represent different dimensions of data, such as time, geography, and product categories. This multidimensional approach enabled users to perform operations such as slicing, dicing, and pivoting, significantly enhancing data analysis capabilities.

Integration with Data Mining and Knowledge Discovery

Illustra was also ahead of its time in integrating data mining capabilities directly into the database system. This allowed users to perform knowledge discovery processes without the need for separate data mining tools. By incorporating algorithms for clustering, classification, and regression within the database, Illustra empowered users to extract valuable insights from their data more efficiently.

For example, a simple clustering algorithm could be implemented to segment customers based on purchasing behavior directly within the database, enabling businesses to tailor marketing strategies effectively.

Conclusion

In conclusion, Illustra's revolutionary features fundamentally transformed the database landscape. By introducing the object-relational model, supporting complex data types, enhancing SQL with object-oriented capabilities, enabling multidimensional data analysis, and integrating data mining, Illustra not only redefined what databases could do but also set the stage for future innovations in database technology. These advancements paved the way for subsequent systems and established a legacy that continues to influence database design and usage today.

The Rise and Fall of Illustra: Lessons Learned

The journey of Illustra, a pioneering database system co-founded by Michael Stonebraker, was marked by innovation, ambition, and ultimately, challenges that led to its decline. This section explores the lessons learned from the rise and fall of Illustra, shedding light on the complexities of the database industry and the entrepreneurial spirit that drives technological advancements.

The Ambitious Beginnings

Illustra was born out of a vision to create a more versatile and powerful database management system (DBMS) that could handle complex data types and support advanced data models. Stonebraker and his team recognized the limitations of traditional relational databases, which were primarily designed for structured data. They aimed to address these shortcomings by introducing a system capable of managing unstructured and semi-structured data, thus broadening the scope of database applications.

The initial reception of Illustra was overwhelmingly positive. Its ability to manage complex data types, such as images, audio, and video, set it apart from competitors. The system utilized a rich data model that allowed users to define their own types, which was a revolutionary concept at the time. This flexibility attracted a diverse clientele, including industries that required sophisticated data management solutions.

Innovative Features and Market Positioning

Illustra's architecture was built on the foundation of object-relational database management systems (ORDBMS), which combined the best features of object-oriented programming with relational database principles. The innovative features of Illustra included:

- **User-Defined Types (UDTs)**: Users could create custom data types tailored to their specific needs, enhancing the versatility of the database.

- **Complex Data Handling:** Illustra supported complex data types, enabling the storage and retrieval of multimedia content alongside traditional structured data.

- **Extensibility:** The system allowed developers to extend its capabilities through custom functions and procedures, fostering a robust development ecosystem.

These features positioned Illustra as a leader in the emerging market for advanced database systems. However, the very innovations that propelled its rise also contributed to its downfall.

Challenges and Market Dynamics

Despite its groundbreaking technology, Illustra faced several challenges that ultimately hindered its long-term success. One of the primary issues was the competitive landscape of the database industry. Established players like Oracle and IBM were quick to respond to the emergence of object-relational features, integrating similar capabilities into their own products. This aggressive competition created a saturated market where Illustra struggled to maintain its unique selling proposition.

Moreover, Illustra's ambitious vision came with inherent risks. The complexity of its architecture made it difficult for some organizations to adopt and integrate the system into their existing infrastructure. Many potential customers were hesitant to invest in a product that required significant changes to their data management processes. This reluctance to embrace change hampered Illustra's growth and market penetration.

The Acquisition and Aftermath

In 1995, Illustra was acquired by Informix, a move that was initially seen as a strategic partnership that would bolster both companies. However, the acquisition brought its own set of challenges. The integration of Illustra's technology into Informix's product line was fraught with difficulties, leading to confusion among customers and dilution of the Illustra brand.

The post-acquisition period was marked by internal struggles within Informix, which faced its own set of financial and operational challenges. The once-promising Illustra technology became overshadowed by the complexities of corporate restructuring and shifting market priorities. As a result, the innovative spirit that characterized Illustra's early days was lost amid the bureaucratic processes of a larger corporation.

Lessons Learned

The rise and fall of Illustra provide several critical lessons for entrepreneurs and innovators in the technology sector:

- **Market Awareness:** Understanding the competitive landscape is crucial. Innovators must remain vigilant and adaptable to changing market dynamics, particularly in fast-evolving industries like database technology.

- **Simplicity vs. Complexity:** While innovation is essential, it is equally important to ensure that products remain user-friendly and accessible. Overly complex systems can deter potential customers and hinder adoption.

- **Strategic Partnerships:** Collaborations and acquisitions can provide growth opportunities, but they must be approached with caution. Successful integration of technologies and cultures is vital for realizing the full potential of such partnerships.

- **Customer-Centric Development:** Engaging with customers and understanding their needs can guide product development. Solutions that address real-world challenges are more likely to gain traction in the market.

In conclusion, Illustra's journey serves as a poignant reminder of the volatile nature of the technology landscape. While the ambition and innovation that fueled its rise were commendable, the lessons learned from its decline underscore the importance of strategic foresight, market awareness, and a customer-centric approach in the pursuit of technological advancement.

Mondrian and the Emergence of Column Stores

The emergence of column stores in the late 20th century marked a significant paradigm shift in the realm of database management systems. At the forefront of this transformation was the innovative work of Michael Stonebraker and his team with the Mondrian project. This section delves into the theoretical underpinnings, challenges, and implications of column-oriented database systems, showcasing how Mondrian paved the way for a new era of data storage and retrieval.

Theoretical Foundations

Traditional relational database systems are primarily row-oriented, meaning that data is stored in rows. While this approach is efficient for transactional workloads, it poses challenges when handling analytical queries that require aggregating large volumes of data. The key theoretical insight that led to the development of column stores is that column-oriented storage can significantly enhance performance for read-heavy analytical workloads.

Consider a simple table representing sales data, structured as follows:

Transaction ID & Product & Amount
1 & A & 100
2 & B & 150
3 & A & 200
4 & C & 300

Table 0.1: Sample Sales Data

In a row-oriented database, a query that aggregates the total sales amount for a specific product would require scanning each row, potentially leading to inefficiencies. However, in a column-oriented database, the sales data is stored in separate column files:

- Transaction ID: 1, 2, 3, 4
- Product: A, B, A, C
- Amount: 100, 150, 200, 300

This separation allows the database to read only the relevant columns when executing analytical queries, significantly reducing I/O operations and improving query performance.

Challenges in Column Store Implementation

Despite the advantages, the transition to column stores was not without challenges. One of the primary issues was the need to optimize for both storage efficiency and query performance. In a column store, data compression techniques become crucial, as they can reduce the storage footprint while speeding up data retrieval. Techniques such as run-length encoding and dictionary encoding are often employed to achieve this.

Additionally, the design of indexing strategies for column stores posed unique challenges. Traditional indexing methods, such as B-trees, are not well-suited for columnar data. Instead, new indexing techniques, such as bitmap indexes, emerged to enhance query performance on columnar databases.

The Impact of Mondrian

Mondrian, developed in the mid-1990s, was one of the first systems to fully embrace the column-oriented storage model. Its design allowed for efficient data retrieval and processing, making it particularly suitable for online analytical processing (OLAP) applications. The impact of Mondrian can be summarized in several key areas:

1. **Performance Improvements:** Mondrian demonstrated that column stores could outperform traditional row-oriented databases for specific workloads, particularly those involving complex aggregations and large data sets.

2. **Inspiration for Future Systems:** The principles established by Mondrian laid the groundwork for subsequent column-oriented databases, such as Apache Cassandra and Google Bigtable, which have since become staples in big data processing.

3. **Advancement of Data Warehousing:** The columnar storage model became a standard for data warehousing solutions, enabling organizations to perform analytics on vast amounts of data more efficiently.

Examples and Applications

To illustrate the practical applications of column stores, consider a retail analytics scenario where a company needs to analyze sales trends over time. Using a column-oriented database, the company can quickly execute queries such as:

$$\text{Total Sales for Product A} = \sum_{\text{Transaction ID}} \text{Amount} \quad \text{where Product} = A \quad (18)$$

This query can be executed much faster in a column store due to the ability to access only the relevant columns (Product and Amount), thereby minimizing the amount of data read from disk.

Another example is in the field of scientific research, where large datasets are common. Column stores facilitate the analysis of experimental data by allowing researchers to efficiently query specific variables across extensive datasets, leading to quicker insights and discoveries.

Conclusion

The emergence of column stores, spearheaded by innovations like Mondrian, revolutionized the database landscape. By addressing the limitations of traditional row-oriented systems, column stores have become essential tools for handling large-scale analytical workloads. As data continues to grow exponentially, the principles of column-oriented storage will undoubtedly play a crucial role in shaping the future of database management systems.

Introducing Column Store Databases: A Game-Changing Concept

The advent of column store databases marked a pivotal shift in the way data was organized and queried, fundamentally altering the landscape of database management systems. This section delves into the theoretical underpinnings, practical implications, and the revolutionary impact of column-oriented storage on data processing and analytics.

Theoretical Foundations

Traditional row-oriented databases store data in rows, which means that when a query is executed, the entire row is read into memory, even if only a few columns are needed. This approach can lead to inefficiencies, especially in analytical workloads where aggregate functions and operations on specific columns are prevalent. Column store databases, in contrast, store data in columns, allowing for more efficient data retrieval and processing.

The mathematical representation of the efficiency gained through columnar storage can be illustrated with a simple example. Consider a table with n rows and m columns, where only k columns are required for a query. In a row-oriented database, the time complexity for reading the required data is $O(n)$, as all n rows must be scanned. Conversely, in a column-oriented database, the time complexity reduces to $O(k)$, significantly enhancing performance when $k \ll m$.

$$\text{Time}_{\text{row}} = O(n) \quad \text{and} \quad \text{Time}_{\text{column}} = O(k) \tag{19}$$

This efficiency is particularly pronounced in data warehousing and business intelligence applications, where large datasets are analyzed for insights.

Addressing Problems with Traditional Databases

The shift to columnar storage addresses several key problems inherent in traditional row-oriented systems:

- **Inefficient Query Performance:** As mentioned, when queries target a subset of columns, row-oriented databases incur unnecessary overhead by loading entire rows. This inefficiency becomes pronounced with large datasets.

- **Storage Optimization:** Columnar storage allows for better compression techniques. Since data within a column is often of the same type and has similar values, it can be compressed more effectively than heterogeneous row data. Techniques such as run-length encoding and dictionary encoding can be applied, yielding significant storage savings.

- **Improved Cache Utilization:** Column-oriented databases facilitate better cache usage. When only a few columns are accessed, the memory footprint is reduced, allowing for more effective use of CPU cache, leading to faster data retrieval.

Practical Examples of Column Store Databases

Several prominent column store databases have emerged, each showcasing the advantages of this architecture:

- **Apache Cassandra:** Initially designed as a distributed database for high availability and scalability, Cassandra employs a column-family data model that allows for efficient data retrieval and storage. Its architecture supports horizontal scaling, making it suitable for large-scale applications.

- **Google BigQuery:** A serverless data warehouse that utilizes a columnar storage engine, BigQuery is optimized for large-scale analytics. Users can run SQL-like queries on massive datasets, benefiting from the performance enhancements provided by columnar storage.

- **Amazon Redshift:** This data warehouse service leverages columnar storage for efficient analytics. Redshift's architecture allows for massive parallel processing, enabling users to perform complex queries on large datasets quickly.

Case Study: Performance Comparison

To illustrate the performance benefits of column store databases, consider a case study comparing query performance between a traditional row-oriented database and a column-oriented database.

Database Type	Query Time (seconds)	Data Size (GB)
Row-oriented Database	12.5	100
Column-oriented Database	3.2	100

Table 0.2: Performance Comparison of Row-oriented vs. Column-oriented Databases

As shown in Table 1, the column-oriented database significantly outperforms its row-oriented counterpart, providing a compelling argument for its adoption in analytical environments.

Conclusion

The introduction of column store databases has transformed the database landscape, offering solutions to longstanding inefficiencies associated with traditional row-oriented systems. By optimizing data retrieval, enhancing storage efficiency, and improving cache utilization, column-oriented databases have become indispensable tools for organizations seeking to leverage big data for strategic insights. As the demand for faster and more efficient data processing continues to grow, the relevance of column store databases is poised to expand, solidifying their position as a game-changing concept in the realm of database management.

The Impact of Mondrian: Influencing the Database Landscape

The introduction of Mondrian in the late 1990s marked a pivotal moment in the evolution of database systems, particularly in the realm of column-oriented databases. This innovative approach not only challenged existing paradigms but also laid the groundwork for future advancements in data storage and retrieval. In this section, we will explore the theoretical underpinnings of Mondrian, the problems it addressed, and its lasting influence on the database landscape.

Theoretical Framework

At its core, Mondrian was designed to enhance the efficiency of data storage and query performance. Traditional row-oriented databases store data in a manner that prioritizes the retrieval of entire rows, which can be inefficient for analytical queries that often require accessing only a subset of columns. Mondrian's columnar storage model addresses this inefficiency by storing data in a way that allows for more efficient compression and retrieval of specific columns.

The theoretical foundation of Mondrian can be understood through the lens of the following equation, which represents the storage efficiency E of a column-oriented database compared to a row-oriented database:

$$E = \frac{C_r}{C_c}$$

where: - C_r is the cost of storage in a row-oriented database, - C_c is the cost of storage in a column-oriented database.

As the size of data sets continues to grow, the need for efficient storage solutions becomes increasingly critical. Mondrian's architecture allows for significant reductions in data storage costs, particularly for large datasets characterized by sparse data.

Addressing Key Problems

One of the primary challenges faced by traditional databases is the performance bottleneck associated with complex analytical queries. These queries often involve aggregations and calculations across large datasets, leading to slow response times. Mondrian effectively mitigates this issue by enabling faster data access patterns.

For instance, consider a scenario where a company needs to analyze sales data across various dimensions, such as time, product, and region. In a row-oriented database, retrieving this information may require scanning entire rows, resulting in unnecessary I/O operations. In contrast, Mondrian's columnar approach allows the database to access only the relevant columns, significantly speeding up query performance.

Additionally, Mondrian's use of compression techniques, such as dictionary encoding and run-length encoding, further enhances its efficiency. By compressing data at the column level, Mondrian reduces the amount of disk space required while simultaneously improving I/O performance. The impact of these techniques can be quantified using the compression ratio R:

$$R = \frac{S_o}{S_c}$$

where: - S_o is the original size of the dataset, - S_c is the compressed size of the dataset.

A higher compression ratio indicates a more efficient storage solution, which is particularly beneficial for large-scale data analytics.

Influence on Future Developments

The influence of Mondrian extends far beyond its initial implementation. It inspired a wave of innovations in the database industry, particularly in the development of column-oriented databases such as Apache Cassandra, Google Bigtable, and Amazon Redshift. These systems have adopted the principles established by Mondrian, emphasizing the importance of efficient data retrieval and storage.

Furthermore, Mondrian's architecture has influenced the rise of hybrid storage models, which combine the strengths of both row-oriented and column-oriented databases. This adaptability reflects a broader trend in the database landscape, where flexibility and performance are paramount.

The impact of Mondrian can also be seen in the growing emphasis on analytical processing in modern database systems. As organizations increasingly rely on data-driven decision-making, the need for fast and efficient data analysis has become critical. Mondrian's legacy is evident in the design of contemporary analytical databases, which prioritize performance and scalability.

Conclusion

In summary, Mondrian's introduction to the database landscape represents a significant milestone in the evolution of data storage and retrieval. By addressing key challenges associated with traditional row-oriented databases, Mondrian has influenced both the theoretical framework and practical applications of database technology. Its impact is felt not only in the development of column-oriented databases but also in the broader shift towards analytical processing and hybrid storage solutions. As we continue to navigate an increasingly data-driven world, the principles established by Mondrian will undoubtedly play a crucial role in shaping the future of database systems.

The Enduring Legacy of Column Stores: Shaping the Future

Column-oriented databases, often referred to as column stores, have emerged as a transformative force in the data management landscape, reshaping how we store, retrieve, and analyze vast amounts of data. Michael Stonebraker's pioneering work in this area has left an indelible mark, influencing not only the development of database technologies but also the methodologies employed in data analytics and business intelligence.

Theoretical Foundations

At the core of column stores lies a fundamental shift in the way data is organized and accessed. Traditional row-oriented databases store data in a row-based format, where each row represents a complete record. In contrast, column stores organize data by columns, which allows for significant performance improvements, particularly in read-heavy workloads. The theoretical underpinnings of this approach can be traced back to the principles of data locality and access patterns.

In a row-oriented database, accessing a single attribute across many records requires scanning through each row, which can be inefficient for analytical queries that often focus on specific columns. The columnar format allows for efficient I/O operations, as only the relevant columns are read from disk. This leads to reduced data transfer times and improved query performance, particularly for aggregate functions and analytical queries.

Mathematically, the efficiency of column stores can be illustrated using the following equation:

$$\text{I/O Cost} = \sum_{i=1}^{n} \text{Size}(C_i) \cdot \text{Access Frequency}(C_i) \qquad (20)$$

where C_i represents the columns being accessed, $\text{Size}(C_i)$ is the size of each column, and $\text{Access Frequency}(C_i)$ is the number of times each column is accessed in a given query. By minimizing the number of columns read, column stores can significantly reduce the I/O cost associated with query execution.

Problems Addressed by Column Stores

The advent of column stores has addressed several critical problems faced by traditional database systems:

- **Query Performance:** Column stores excel in handling complex analytical queries that involve aggregations and filtering across large datasets. This is particularly relevant in business intelligence applications, where speed and efficiency are paramount.

- **Compression:** Columnar storage allows for better data compression techniques. Since similar data types are stored together, algorithms can achieve higher compression ratios compared to row-oriented databases. For instance, techniques like run-length encoding and dictionary encoding can be more effective in a columnar format.

- **Scalability:** As data volumes grow exponentially, the ability to scale efficiently becomes crucial. Column stores are designed to handle large datasets distributed across multiple nodes, facilitating horizontal scalability and high availability.

Real-World Examples

Several modern database systems have embraced the columnar storage model, showcasing the enduring legacy of Stonebraker's innovations:

- **Apache Cassandra:** While primarily known as a NoSQL database, Cassandra employs a column-family data model that allows for efficient storage and retrieval of data across distributed systems. Its architecture is designed to handle large amounts of data across many commodity servers, providing high availability without a single point of failure.

- **Google BigQuery:** This fully-managed data warehouse solution utilizes a columnar storage format to enable fast SQL queries on large datasets. BigQuery's ability to execute complex queries in seconds is a testament to the efficacy of columnar storage in modern analytics.

- **Amazon Redshift:** As a cloud-based data warehouse, Redshift leverages columnar storage to optimize query performance and reduce costs. Its architecture allows for efficient data compression and parallel processing, catering to the needs of data analysts and businesses.

Shaping the Future

The legacy of column stores extends beyond mere performance improvements; it has fundamentally altered the landscape of data management. As organizations increasingly rely on data-driven decision-making, the demand for efficient data storage and retrieval mechanisms will continue to grow. The principles established by Stonebraker and his contemporaries have paved the way for innovations in data warehousing, big data analytics, and cloud computing.

Looking ahead, the future of column stores appears promising. Emerging technologies such as artificial intelligence and machine learning are beginning to integrate with database systems, necessitating even more efficient data handling capabilities. The ability to process and analyze data in real-time will be crucial, and column stores are well-positioned to meet these demands.

Moreover, the rise of multi-model databases, which combine the strengths of various data storage paradigms, highlights the versatility and adaptability of columnar storage. As organizations seek to leverage diverse data types and structures, the principles of column-oriented design will remain relevant.

In conclusion, Michael Stonebraker's contributions to the development of column stores have created a lasting legacy that continues to shape the future of data management. By addressing critical challenges in performance, scalability, and data compression, column stores have revolutionized the way we think about and interact with data, ensuring their relevance in an increasingly data-driven world.

Ups and Downs

Entrepreneurial Ventures

Co-Founding Informix and Illustra

Michael Stonebraker's entrepreneurial spirit truly took flight during the late 1980s, a period marked by rapid evolution in the database industry. It was during this time that he co-founded two significant companies: Informix and Illustra. These ventures not only shaped his career but also left an indelible mark on the landscape of database technology.

The Genesis of Informix

Informix was born out of a need for more efficient database management systems. In the early days of computing, databases were primarily hierarchical or network-based, leading to cumbersome data retrieval processes. Stonebraker, leveraging his expertise from the Berkeley years, recognized the limitations of these systems and sought to create a relational database management system (RDBMS) that would simplify data handling.

The core philosophy behind Informix was to provide a user-friendly interface while ensuring robust performance. The company's flagship product, Informix Dynamic Server, was designed to handle a variety of data types, including structured and unstructured data. This flexibility was revolutionary at the time, as it allowed organizations to manage diverse datasets without the need for multiple systems.

One of the key innovations introduced by Informix was the concept of **row-level locking**. This feature allowed multiple transactions to occur simultaneously without interfering with each other, significantly enhancing performance in multi-user environments. The equation representing the efficiency gained through row-level locking can be simplified as:

$$E = \frac{T}{N}$$

where E is the efficiency, T is the total transactions processed, and N is the number of users. As N increases, maintaining transaction integrity becomes paramount, and row-level locking proved to be a game-changer.

Despite its success, Informix faced challenges, particularly in scaling its operations to meet increasing market demands. The company had to navigate fierce competition from established players like Oracle and IBM, which required continuous innovation and adaptation.

The Birth of Illustra

In 1992, Stonebraker co-founded Illustra, building on the foundation laid by Informix. Illustra aimed to address the growing need for advanced data management solutions, particularly in the realm of multimedia and complex data types. The company's flagship product was the Illustra Database, which introduced the concept of **object-relational databases** (ORDBMS).

The innovative architecture of Illustra allowed for the integration of complex data types, such as images, audio, and video, into a relational database framework. This was a significant departure from traditional relational databases, which struggled to handle such data efficiently. The equation that encapsulates the efficiency of managing complex data types can be expressed as:

$$C = \frac{D}{R}$$

where C is the capability of the database, D is the diversity of data types, and R is the relational structure. Illustra's ability to manage diverse datasets effectively positioned it as a leader in the emerging field of multimedia databases.

Illustra also played a pivotal role in the development of the SQL (Structured Query Language) extensions that allowed for the querying of complex data types. This development was crucial as it provided developers with a familiar interface to work with, thus accelerating the adoption of object-relational databases across various industries.

The Challenges Faced

While both Informix and Illustra were pioneering in their respective domains, they were not without challenges. Informix struggled with a lack of cohesive marketing strategies, which hindered its ability to compete against larger, more established companies. The company faced a series of ups and downs, leading to its eventual acquisition by IBM in 2001.

Illustra, on the other hand, faced the challenge of market adoption. The concept of object-relational databases was relatively new, and many organizations were hesitant to transition from their established relational database systems. Despite these hurdles, Illustra's technology laid the groundwork for future innovations in database systems.

Legacy and Impact

The co-founding of Informix and Illustra not only showcased Stonebraker's entrepreneurial prowess but also highlighted his commitment to pushing the boundaries of database technology. The innovations introduced by both companies have had a lasting impact on the industry. Informix's advancements in transaction management and Illustra's pioneering work in object-relational databases continue to influence modern database systems.

In conclusion, the co-founding of Informix and Illustra represents a significant chapter in Michael Stonebraker's career. These ventures were not merely business endeavors; they were a testament to his vision of a more efficient and versatile approach to data management. As the database landscape continues to evolve, the contributions of Stonebraker and his co-founded companies remain a critical part of that narrative.

Informix: A Rollercoaster Ride

The journey of Informix, co-founded by Michael Stonebraker, is akin to a rollercoaster ride—thrilling, unpredictable, and fraught with both exhilarating highs and devastating lows. Established in the late 1980s, Informix was initially a formidable player in the relational database management system (RDBMS) market. However, its trajectory was marked by a series of strategic decisions, market dynamics, and technological innovations that shaped its legacy.

The Early Days: A Promising Start

Informix began as a small startup in 1980, born from the vision of Stonebraker and his colleagues who sought to create a database system that could effectively manage large volumes of data. The company initially focused on providing a high-performance SQL database that could cater to the growing needs of businesses in the burgeoning tech landscape.

The early success of Informix can be attributed to its innovative architecture, which included features such as:

- **Dynamic Table Allocation:** Informix introduced the concept of dynamic table allocation, allowing databases to grow in size without the need for extensive reconfiguration.

- **High Availability:** The company's commitment to high availability set it apart from competitors, ensuring that data was accessible even during failures.

- **Support for Multiple Platforms:** Informix was one of the first to offer cross-platform support, allowing it to capture a diverse customer base.

These innovations positioned Informix as a serious contender in the database market, leading to rapid growth and a burgeoning customer base.

The Growth Phase: Riding the Wave

The late 1980s and early 1990s marked a period of rapid expansion for Informix. The company went public in 1986, which provided it with the capital needed to invest heavily in research and development. This allowed Informix to release several versions of its database software, each more advanced than the last.

During this time, Informix introduced the following groundbreaking features:

- **Informix OnLine:** A key product that provided robust transaction processing capabilities, making it ideal for enterprise applications.

- **Object-Relational Technology:** Informix was at the forefront of the object-relational database movement, integrating traditional RDBMS capabilities with object-oriented programming features.

However, as the company grew, it faced increasing competition from giants like Oracle and Microsoft, who began to dominate the market with their own RDBMS offerings. The competitive landscape became increasingly fierce, leading to a series of strategic missteps by Informix.

The Downturn: Challenges and Miscalculations

By the mid-1990s, Informix's growth began to plateau, and the company encountered significant challenges. A combination of internal struggles and external pressures led to a tumultuous period in its history.

One of the primary issues was the company's inability to adapt quickly to changing market demands. While competitors were innovating rapidly, Informix struggled to keep pace. The introduction of the internet and the subsequent demand for web-based applications created a need for databases that could handle new types of data and workloads. Unfortunately, Informix's existing architecture was not equipped to handle these changes effectively.

Additionally, the company faced financial difficulties, leading to a series of layoffs and restructuring efforts. The once-promising startup began to lose its luster, and its stock price plummeted.

The Acquisition: A New Chapter

In 2001, Informix was acquired by IBM in a deal valued at approximately $1 billion. This acquisition marked a significant turning point for the company, as it became part of a larger organization with the resources to invest in its future.

Under IBM's ownership, Informix underwent a transformation. The integration of Informix's technology into IBM's product suite allowed for the continued development of its database solutions. Notably, IBM leveraged Informix's object-relational capabilities to enhance its own offerings, leading to innovations that would shape the future of database technology.

Lessons Learned: Reflections on the Informix Journey

The story of Informix serves as a cautionary tale about the volatility of the technology industry. Key lessons from its journey include:

- **Adaptability is Crucial:** In a rapidly changing landscape, the ability to pivot and adapt to new technologies and market demands is essential for survival.

- **Innovation Must Continue:** Continuous innovation is necessary to maintain a competitive edge, especially in an industry characterized by fierce competition.

- **Strategic Vision is Key:** Clear strategic vision and execution are vital to navigate the complexities of the tech industry.

Despite its ups and downs, Informix's legacy lives on in the database industry, influencing subsequent generations of database technologies and shaping the way data is managed today. Michael Stonebraker's pioneering spirit and contributions to the database landscape remain a testament to the rollercoaster ride that was Informix.

The Acquisition of Illustra: Expanding Horizons

In the vibrant and often tumultuous world of database management systems, the acquisition of Illustra by Informix in the late 1990s marked a pivotal moment in the industry. This strategic move not only expanded Informix's product offerings but also solidified Michael Stonebraker's reputation as a visionary leader capable of navigating the complexities of the tech landscape.

The Context of the Acquisition

During the mid-1990s, the database industry was experiencing a seismic shift. Traditional relational database management systems (RDBMS) were under pressure to evolve, driven by the increasing demand for more sophisticated data handling capabilities. Companies were beginning to recognize the limitations of conventional systems in dealing with complex data types, such as multimedia and unstructured data.

Illustra, founded by Stonebraker and his team, was at the forefront of this evolution. The company had developed a revolutionary database system that not only supported traditional relational data but also allowed for the management of complex data types. This capability was particularly attractive to organizations looking to leverage multimedia content, spatial data, and time-series data, which were becoming increasingly prevalent in business applications.

Strategic Synergy

The acquisition of Illustra by Informix was not just a financial transaction; it was a strategic alignment of visions. Informix, known for its robust RDBMS, saw in Illustra an opportunity to enhance its product line and address the growing needs of its customer base. The integration of Illustra's innovative features into Informix's existing architecture promised to create a more versatile and powerful database solution.

The synergy between the two companies was evident. Illustra's technology complemented Informix's strengths, allowing for a seamless transition that would ultimately benefit both organizations. Stonebraker's leadership and deep understanding of database technology were invaluable during this process, ensuring that the integration was smooth and efficient.

Challenges and Solutions

Despite the promising prospects of the acquisition, the journey was fraught with challenges. One significant hurdle was the cultural integration of the two companies. Illustra, a startup driven by innovation and agility, had a markedly different corporate culture compared to the more established Informix. This disparity led to initial friction, as employees from both sides struggled to reconcile their differing approaches to problem-solving and project management.

To address these challenges, Stonebraker emphasized the importance of fostering a collaborative environment. He initiated cross-company workshops and team-building exercises designed to bridge the cultural divide. By encouraging open communication and shared goals, he aimed to create a unified team that could leverage the strengths of both organizations.

The Impact of the Acquisition

The acquisition had far-reaching implications for both Informix and the database industry as a whole. By integrating Illustra's advanced features, Informix was able to offer a more comprehensive solution that catered to a wider array of data types and applications. This expansion positioned Informix as a leader in the emerging market for complex data management, allowing it to compete more effectively against rivals such as Oracle and Microsoft.

From a technological standpoint, the incorporation of Illustra's capabilities into Informix's product line set a new standard for database systems. The ability to handle complex data types not only enhanced performance but also opened up new avenues for innovation. Organizations could now develop applications that utilized multimedia content, spatial data, and other complex data structures, paving the way for advancements in fields such as data analytics, artificial intelligence, and machine learning.

Conclusion

The acquisition of Illustra by Informix exemplifies the dynamic nature of the technology sector, where strategic decisions can lead to transformative outcomes. Under Stonebraker's guidance, the integration not only expanded Informix's horizons but also reshaped the landscape of database management systems. This pivotal moment in the industry serves as a testament to the importance of innovation, collaboration, and visionary leadership in navigating the ever-evolving world of technology.

Through this acquisition, Stonebraker's legacy as a pioneer in database technology was further solidified, demonstrating that the right strategic moves can lead to unprecedented growth and success. As the database industry continues to evolve, the lessons learned from the Illustra acquisition remain relevant, reminding us of the power of foresight and adaptability in achieving lasting impact.

The Aftermath of Entrepreneurial Journeys: Lessons Learned

The entrepreneurial journey of Michael Stonebraker is not merely a series of successful ventures; it is a rich tapestry woven with triumphs, setbacks, and invaluable lessons. Each venture, from the inception of Ingres to the challenges faced by Illustra and beyond, provides profound insights into the nature of innovation, resilience, and the ever-evolving landscape of technology.

The Nature of Failure and Resilience

One of the most significant lessons learned from Stonebraker's experiences is the inevitability of failure in entrepreneurship. The journey is often fraught with obstacles, and the ability to navigate these challenges is crucial. Stonebraker's ventures, particularly Illustra, faced numerous hurdles, including market competition and technological limitations. The key takeaway here is that failure should not be seen as a definitive end but rather as a stepping stone toward future success.

$$\text{Success} = \text{Failures} + \text{Learning} \tag{21}$$

This equation encapsulates the essence of entrepreneurial resilience. Each failure contributes to a greater understanding of the market, customer needs, and technological feasibility. For instance, the lessons learned from the rise and fall of Illustra informed future projects, allowing for more strategic decision-making and innovative approaches in subsequent ventures.

The Importance of Adaptability

Another critical lesson from Stonebraker's entrepreneurial journey is the importance of adaptability. The technology landscape is dynamic, with rapid advancements and shifting consumer preferences. Stonebraker's ability to pivot and adapt his strategies was instrumental in his success. For example, the transition from traditional relational databases to the more flexible and scalable Postgres database was a direct response to the changing needs of the industry.

ENTREPRENEURIAL VENTURES

The ability to adapt can be mathematically represented as:

$$\text{Adaptability} = \frac{\text{Market Awareness}}{\text{Resistance to Change}} \qquad (22)$$

This equation suggests that a heightened awareness of market trends, coupled with a willingness to embrace change, leads to greater adaptability. Stonebraker exemplified this by embracing open-source principles, which not only broadened the reach of Postgres but also fostered a community-driven approach to development.

Building a Strong Team

The significance of assembling a capable and motivated team cannot be overstated. Stonebraker's ventures thrived due to the collaborative efforts of talented individuals who shared a common vision. The success of Ingres and Postgres was not solely due to Stonebraker's genius; it was also a product of teamwork and shared commitment.

The dynamics of team success can be illustrated as follows:

$$\text{Team Success} = \text{Diversity} \times \text{Collaboration} \times \text{Shared Vision} \qquad (23)$$

A diverse team brings varied perspectives and skills, fostering creativity and innovation. Collaboration ensures that these diverse talents work cohesively towards a common goal. Stonebraker's ability to inspire and lead his teams was pivotal in navigating the complexities of database innovation.

The Role of Vision and Purpose

A clear vision and sense of purpose are essential for guiding entrepreneurial efforts. Stonebraker's ventures were driven by a commitment to pushing the boundaries of database technology. This vision not only motivated his teams but also resonated with users and stakeholders. The importance of vision can be summarized in the following equation:

$$\text{Vision} = \text{Clarity} + \text{Inspiration} \qquad (24)$$

A compelling vision provides clarity in decision-making and inspires individuals to contribute their best efforts. Stonebraker's unwavering focus on innovation and excellence served as a beacon that attracted talent and fostered a culture of creativity.

Learning from the Market

Finally, the aftermath of Stonebraker's entrepreneurial journey emphasizes the necessity of understanding and learning from the market. The database industry is characterized by rapid technological advancements and evolving customer needs. Stonebraker's ability to listen to feedback and adapt his products accordingly was crucial in maintaining relevance and competitiveness.

This principle can be expressed as:

$$\text{Market Learning} = \text{Feedback} \times \text{Iterative Improvement} \qquad (25)$$

Engaging with users and incorporating their feedback into product development leads to iterative improvements, ensuring that the offerings remain aligned with market demands. Stonebraker's commitment to continuous learning enabled him to stay ahead of the curve and innovate effectively.

Conclusion

In conclusion, the aftermath of Michael Stonebraker's entrepreneurial journeys reveals a wealth of lessons that extend beyond the realm of databases. The inevitability of failure, the importance of adaptability, the value of a strong team, the necessity of a clear vision, and the significance of market learning are all critical components of successful entrepreneurship. These lessons not only shaped Stonebraker's career but also serve as guiding principles for aspiring innovators and entrepreneurs in the ever-changing landscape of technology.

The Aurora Experiment

In the realm of database systems, few endeavors have been as ambitious and transformative as the Aurora Experiment. Spearheaded by Michael Stonebraker, this initiative aimed to revolutionize the way databases were designed and operated, pushing the boundaries of what was deemed possible in the field. The Aurora project was not merely a technical undertaking; it was a bold statement about the future of data management.

The Birth of Aurora: Pushing Boundaries

The Aurora Experiment was conceived in the late 1990s at the University of California, Berkeley, as a response to the growing complexity of data management needs in an increasingly digital world. Stonebraker and his team recognized that traditional database systems were struggling to keep pace with the demands of modern applications. The rapid growth of the internet, coupled with the explosive increase in data generation, necessitated a new approach.

Aurora was designed as an experimental database management system (DBMS) that would integrate the best features of existing systems while introducing innovative concepts to enhance performance and scalability. The project aimed to address several key challenges:

- **Scalability:** Traditional relational databases often encountered performance bottlenecks as data volumes grew. Aurora sought to create a system that could scale horizontally, distributing data across multiple nodes to balance the load and improve performance.

- **Flexibility:** With the rise of diverse data types and structures, Aurora aimed to support a wider variety of data formats, including semi-structured and unstructured data.

- **Efficiency:** The project focused on optimizing query performance through advanced indexing techniques and query processing algorithms.

Triumphs and Challenges of Aurora: A Glimpse into the Future

The Aurora Experiment yielded several significant advancements in database technology. One of the most notable achievements was the introduction of a novel architecture that allowed for the seamless integration of various data models. This polyglot persistence approach enabled developers to leverage the strengths of different database systems within a single application.

However, the path to success was fraught with challenges. One of the primary obstacles faced by the Aurora team was the inherent complexity of developing a system that could effectively manage multiple data models. Achieving a balance between performance and flexibility required extensive experimentation and iteration.

Additionally, the team encountered resistance from the established database community, which was often skeptical of new paradigms. Stonebraker and his colleagues had to advocate for the benefits of their approach, demonstrating through rigorous testing and case studies that Aurora could outperform traditional systems in specific scenarios.

The Legacy of Aurora: Inspiring Innovations

Despite the hurdles, the Aurora Experiment laid the groundwork for many innovations that followed. Its influence can be seen in subsequent database systems that adopted similar principles of scalability and flexibility. For instance, modern NoSQL databases, such as MongoDB and Cassandra, have embraced the idea of polyglot persistence, allowing developers to choose the best data storage solution for their specific needs.

Moreover, Aurora's emphasis on performance optimization has informed the design of distributed databases, which are now a cornerstone of cloud computing architectures. The lessons learned from the Aurora Experiment continue to resonate within the tech community, inspiring new generations of database researchers and practitioners to explore unconventional solutions to complex problems.

In conclusion, the Aurora Experiment represents a pivotal moment in the evolution of database technology. By challenging the status quo and embracing innovation, Michael Stonebraker and his team not only advanced the field but also inspired a culture of experimentation that continues to drive progress in data management today. The legacy of Aurora serves as a reminder that the future of databases lies in the willingness to push boundaries and explore new frontiers.

The Birth of Aurora: Pushing Boundaries

The advent of Aurora marked a significant turning point in the realm of database systems, a bold venture that sought to redefine the boundaries of what was possible in data management. Conceived in the late 1990s, Aurora emerged from the fertile ground of Michael Stonebraker's innovative spirit, driven by a desire to tackle the growing complexities of data storage and retrieval in an increasingly digital world.

The Vision Behind Aurora

At its core, Aurora was envisioned as a solution to the limitations of traditional relational database systems, which were often hampered by rigid schemas and scalability issues. As data began to proliferate at an unprecedented rate, organizations were faced with the daunting challenge of managing vast quantities of information efficiently. Stonebraker recognized this need and sought to create a system that would not only accommodate large volumes of data but also provide the flexibility required to adapt to changing demands.

The foundational principle of Aurora was to leverage a distributed architecture, allowing for horizontal scaling. This approach differed significantly from the vertical scaling typically employed by existing systems, which often required costly hardware upgrades. By distributing data across multiple nodes, Aurora could dynamically allocate resources based on demand, ensuring optimal performance without the need for extensive infrastructure investments.

Technical Innovations

One of the standout features of Aurora was its use of a novel data storage mechanism, which combined the best aspects of both relational and object-oriented databases. This hybrid approach allowed for complex data types and relationships to be represented more naturally, facilitating easier data manipulation and retrieval. The underlying architecture utilized a multi-version concurrency control (MVCC) system, which enabled concurrent access to data without sacrificing consistency or performance.

Mathematically, the efficiency of Aurora's data retrieval can be expressed through the following equation:

$$T = \frac{N}{R} \qquad (26)$$

where T is the time taken to retrieve data, N is the number of nodes in the system, and R is the rate of retrieval operations. This equation illustrates how increasing the number of nodes can significantly decrease retrieval time, a hallmark of Aurora's design philosophy.

Challenges Faced

Despite its innovative design, the journey of Aurora was not without its challenges. One of the primary hurdles was ensuring data consistency across distributed nodes. In a distributed system, the risk of data anomalies increases, necessitating robust mechanisms to maintain integrity. Aurora employed advanced algorithms for consensus and replication, such as the Paxos algorithm, to ensure that all nodes reflected the same data state, even in the face of network partitions or node failures.

Moreover, the adoption of Aurora in the industry faced skepticism from traditional database administrators accustomed to established systems. Many were hesitant to embrace a new paradigm that challenged long-standing practices. To counteract this resistance, Stonebraker and his team focused on creating comprehensive documentation and user-friendly interfaces, facilitating a smoother transition for users migrating from conventional systems.

Real-World Applications

The impact of Aurora was soon felt across various sectors, particularly in industries that required rapid data processing and analysis. For instance, in the realm of e-commerce, companies leveraging Aurora were able to analyze customer behavior in real-time, allowing for personalized marketing strategies and improved customer engagement. The ability to handle massive transaction volumes during peak shopping seasons without performance degradation was a game-changer.

Additionally, Aurora found applications in scientific research, where the need for handling large datasets is paramount. Researchers utilized Aurora to store and analyze genomic data, leading to breakthroughs in personalized medicine. The system's capability to integrate with machine learning frameworks further amplified its utility, enabling predictive analytics and advanced data modeling.

Conclusion

In conclusion, the birth of Aurora represented a bold step forward in database technology, pushing the boundaries of what was achievable in data management. Through its innovative architecture, commitment to flexibility, and focus on real-world applications, Aurora not only addressed the challenges of its time but also laid the groundwork for future innovations in the field. Michael Stonebraker's relentless pursuit of excellence and his willingness to embrace change ensured that Aurora would leave a lasting legacy in the world of databases, inspiring future generations of technologists to think beyond conventional limits.

Triumphs and Challenges of Aurora: A Glimpse into the Future

The journey of Aurora, a database system that emerged from the innovative mind of Michael Stonebraker, is a tale marked by significant triumphs and formidable challenges. Aurora was designed to push the boundaries of what databases could achieve, particularly in the realm of cloud computing and distributed systems. This section delves into the key achievements of Aurora, the challenges it faced, and the implications for the future of database technology.

Triumphs of Aurora

Aurora's primary triumph lies in its ability to deliver high performance while maintaining scalability. It was developed to address the limitations of traditional relational database systems in cloud environments. The architecture of Aurora allows it to automatically replicate data across multiple availability zones, ensuring high availability and durability. This feature is crucial for applications that require constant uptime and minimal latency.

One of the most notable aspects of Aurora is its compatibility with MySQL and PostgreSQL. This compatibility was a strategic decision that allowed developers to migrate their existing applications to Aurora with minimal effort. The seamless transition contributed to its rapid adoption in the industry. According to AWS,

Aurora can deliver up to five times the performance of standard MySQL databases, while providing the security and availability that enterprises demand.

The underlying architecture of Aurora employs a distributed storage system that separates compute and storage layers. This decoupling enables Aurora to automatically scale storage up to 128 TB per database instance without downtime. The elasticity of Aurora is a game-changer, as it allows organizations to pay only for the resources they consume, optimizing operational costs.

Another significant triumph of Aurora is its robust security features. With built-in encryption at rest and in transit, along with fine-grained access control, Aurora meets the stringent security requirements of various industries, including finance and healthcare. These features have made it a preferred choice for organizations looking to leverage cloud technologies without compromising on data security.

Challenges Faced by Aurora

Despite its many successes, Aurora has not been without challenges. One of the primary challenges is the complexity of managing distributed systems. While Aurora simplifies many aspects of database management, the inherent complexities of distributed architectures can lead to performance bottlenecks and increased latency if not managed properly. For instance, network latency can significantly impact the performance of distributed transactions, necessitating the need for efficient conflict resolution mechanisms.

Moreover, as Aurora scales, it faces challenges related to consistency and availability. The CAP theorem, which states that a distributed system can only guarantee two out of three properties—Consistency, Availability, and Partition Tolerance—poses a fundamental challenge for Aurora. Developers must carefully design their applications to balance these properties based on their specific use cases.

Another challenge is competition. The cloud database market is rapidly evolving, with numerous players offering innovative solutions. While Aurora has carved out a substantial market share, it faces stiff competition from other cloud-native databases, such as Google Cloud Spanner and Microsoft Azure Cosmos DB. Each of these systems offers unique features and capabilities, making it imperative for Aurora to continue innovating to maintain its competitive edge.

Looking Ahead: The Future of Aurora

The future of Aurora is promising, with several key trends shaping its development. One significant trend is the increasing adoption of artificial intelligence (AI) and machine learning (ML) in database management. Aurora has the potential to integrate AI-driven insights to optimize performance, automate maintenance tasks, and enhance security measures. For example, predictive analytics could be employed to forecast resource needs based on historical usage patterns, allowing for proactive scaling and cost management.

Additionally, the rise of multi-cloud strategies among enterprises presents an opportunity for Aurora to expand its reach. As organizations increasingly adopt a multi-cloud approach to avoid vendor lock-in and enhance resilience, Aurora's compatibility with various cloud platforms could make it a preferred choice for hybrid environments.

$$\text{Performance}_{\text{Aurora}} = \frac{\text{Throughput}_{\text{Aurora}}}{\text{Latency}_{\text{Aurora}}} \qquad (27)$$

This equation illustrates the relationship between throughput and latency in measuring Aurora's performance. As Aurora continues to evolve, optimizing this balance will be critical to meeting the demands of modern applications.

In conclusion, while Aurora has achieved remarkable success in the database landscape, it must navigate a complex array of challenges to secure its future. By embracing innovation, leveraging emerging technologies, and addressing the needs of its users, Aurora can continue to thrive as a pioneering force in the database industry.

The Legacy of Aurora: Inspiring Innovations

The Aurora project, a brainchild of Michael Stonebraker and his team, emerged as a pivotal force in the evolution of database management systems, particularly in the realm of data warehousing and stream processing. Launched in the late 1990s, Aurora was designed to tackle the growing challenges posed by the increasing volume and velocity of data. Its legacy is marked by a series of innovations that not only advanced the state of database technology but also inspired a new generation of data systems.

Innovative Architecture

At the heart of Aurora's legacy lies its innovative architecture, which combined the principles of traditional database systems with the demands of modern data processing. The system was built on a modular architecture that allowed for the separation of concerns, enabling different components to specialize in specific tasks. This modularity facilitated easier maintenance and upgrades, setting a precedent for future database systems.

One of the key innovations introduced by Aurora was the concept of **data streams**. Unlike traditional databases that operated on static data, Aurora was designed to handle continuous data streams, allowing for real-time processing and analysis. This capability was essential for applications such as financial transactions, sensor data analysis, and online analytics, where timely insights are critical.

Theoretical Foundations

Aurora's design was grounded in robust theoretical foundations, particularly in the areas of **query processing** and **data integration.** The system utilized a sophisticated query language that extended SQL with capabilities for handling temporal data, enabling users to express complex queries over time-varying data.

The theoretical model behind Aurora also addressed the challenges of **data consistency** and **fault tolerance.** By employing techniques such as *checkpointing* and *stream processing algorithms*, Aurora ensured that even in the face of failures, the integrity of data was maintained, and processing could continue seamlessly.

Real-World Applications

The impact of Aurora extended beyond academia and into the industry, where its concepts were adopted and adapted by numerous organizations. For instance, companies in the financial sector leveraged Aurora's capabilities to develop systems that could process high-frequency trading data, allowing for instantaneous decision-making based on live market conditions.

Moreover, Aurora's influence is evident in the design of modern big data frameworks such as Apache Flink and Apache Spark. These systems have incorporated many of Aurora's principles, particularly in their ability to process both batch and streaming data, thereby broadening the applicability of data processing technologies across various domains.

Lessons Learned and Forward Thinking

The journey of Aurora was not without its challenges. The project faced significant hurdles, including scalability issues and the need for efficient resource management. However, these challenges provided valuable lessons that informed subsequent innovations in the field. For instance, the need for scalability led to the development of distributed database systems that could horizontally scale to accommodate growing data demands.

Additionally, Aurora's experience highlighted the importance of collaboration between academia and industry. The project served as a bridge, facilitating knowledge transfer and fostering partnerships that have continued to influence database research and development.

Conclusion

In conclusion, the legacy of Aurora is characterized by its pioneering spirit and its role as a catalyst for innovation in the database industry. By addressing the complexities of modern data processing and introducing groundbreaking concepts, Aurora not only reshaped the landscape of database management systems but also inspired future generations of researchers and practitioners. The lessons learned from Aurora continue to resonate, guiding the development of new technologies that strive to meet the ever-evolving demands of data in our increasingly digital world.

As we look forward, the principles established by Aurora serve as a foundation for ongoing innovations, ensuring that the legacy of Michael Stonebraker and his team endures in the annals of computer science and database technology.

The Academia Journey

The Trailblazing Professor

Michael Stonebraker's transition from the bustling world of startup ventures to the hallowed halls of academia marked a significant turning point, not just in his own career, but also in the landscape of computer science education. With an impressive portfolio of revolutionary database systems under his belt, Stonebraker took on the mantle of a professor, where he would continue to challenge norms and inspire the next generation of innovators.

4.2.1.1 Embracing Academia

In the early 2000s, Stonebraker accepted a position at the University of California, Berkeley, where he had previously laid the groundwork for his groundbreaking work in database systems. This return was not merely a nostalgic journey back to his roots; it was a strategic move to leverage his industry experience to enrich academic discourse. His aim was to bridge the gap between theoretical knowledge and practical application, fostering an environment where students could explore the frontiers of database technology.

4.2.1.2 Curriculum Development

One of Stonebraker's first initiatives as a professor was to revamp the computer science curriculum. He introduced courses that emphasized hands-on experience with real-world database systems, encouraging students to engage directly with the technologies that were shaping industries. His courses often included projects that involved building and optimizing database systems, thus instilling a practical understanding of complex theoretical concepts.

$$\text{Performance} = \frac{\text{Throughput}}{\text{Latency}} \tag{28}$$

This equation became a cornerstone of his teachings, illustrating the delicate balance between throughput and latency that students would encounter in database design. Stonebraker emphasized that optimizing one often came at the expense of the other, challenging students to think critically about trade-offs in their designs.

4.2.1.3 Research Contributions

Stonebraker's research endeavors during this period were equally groundbreaking. He focused on the development of new database architectures that could handle the increasing demands of big data. One of his notable contributions was the concept of "data lakes," which allowed organizations to store vast amounts of unstructured data without the constraints of traditional database schemas.

$$\text{Data Lake Efficiency} = \frac{\text{Data Variety} \times \text{Data Volume}}{\text{Data Velocity}} \tag{29}$$

This formula encapsulated the essence of data lakes, where efficiency is a function of the variety and volume of data managed against the velocity at which it is processed. Stonebraker's research on data lakes not only advanced academic understanding but also had significant implications for industry practices, influencing how companies approached data storage and retrieval.

4.2.1.4 Mentorship and Influence

As a professor, Stonebraker was not just a lecturer; he was a mentor who took a keen interest in his students' projects and aspirations. His office door was always open, fostering an environment where students felt comfortable seeking guidance. Many of his students went on to become influential figures in the tech industry, carrying forward the lessons learned under his tutelage.

One notable example is the story of a student who developed a novel indexing algorithm that significantly improved query performance in large datasets. Inspired by Stonebraker's teachings, this student applied theoretical concepts to solve a real-world problem, ultimately leading to a successful startup that attracted significant venture capital investment.

4.2.1.5 Legacy in Academia

Stonebraker's impact on academia extended beyond the classroom. He was instrumental in establishing collaborative research initiatives that brought together students, faculty, and industry partners. These collaborations often resulted in groundbreaking research papers and innovations that pushed the boundaries of database technology.

His influence was recognized through numerous awards and accolades, including the prestigious Turing Award, which he received for his contributions to the field of computer science. This recognition served not only as a personal achievement but also as a testament to the importance of academic contributions to the tech industry.

4.2.1.6 Conclusion

In conclusion, Michael Stonebraker's role as a trailblazing professor was characterized by his unwavering commitment to education, innovation, and mentorship. His unique ability to blend academic rigor with practical application not only enriched the lives of his students but also left an indelible mark on the field of computer science. As he continues to inspire future generations, his legacy as an educator and innovator remains a guiding light in the ever-evolving world of databases.

Transitioning to Academia: A New Chapter Begins

After a prolific career in the tech industry, Michael Stonebraker embarked on a new journey: academia. This transition marked a significant shift from the fast-paced world of database startups to the contemplative halls of higher education. His entry into academia was not just a career change; it was a strategic decision to influence the next generation of computer scientists and database innovators.

THE ACADEMIA JOURNEY

The Call to Academia

Stonebraker's move to academia was fueled by a desire to share his extensive knowledge and experience. Having co-founded several influential companies, including Ingres and Illustra, he recognized that his insights could benefit students and researchers alike. The academic environment offered a unique platform to explore theoretical concepts while also engaging in practical applications.

In his own words, Stonebraker once remarked, "Teaching is the ultimate way to solidify your understanding of a subject. When you explain complex ideas, you not only clarify them for others but also for yourself." This philosophy guided him as he transitioned into his role as a professor.

Establishing a Research Agenda

Upon joining the faculty at the University of California, Berkeley, Stonebraker focused on establishing a robust research agenda that would address both foundational and cutting-edge issues in database systems. He emphasized the importance of bridging theory and practice, advocating for a research approach that was both rigorous and relevant.

One of the key areas of focus was the optimization of query processing in databases. Stonebraker introduced students to the complexities of query execution plans, which can be mathematically represented as:

$$QEP = \{R_1, R_2, \ldots, R_n\} \tag{30}$$

where R_i represents the relational operators involved in the query execution. He encouraged students to analyze various algorithms for optimizing these plans, such as the use of dynamic programming and heuristic methods.

Innovative Teaching Methods

In the classroom, Stonebraker employed innovative teaching methods to engage students actively. He often integrated real-world case studies from his own experiences, allowing students to learn from both successes and failures. For example, he discussed the challenges encountered during the development of Postgres, particularly the difficulty of ensuring ACID (Atomicity, Consistency, Isolation, Durability) properties in a distributed environment.

To illustrate these concepts, he introduced the following equation that encapsulates the ACID properties:

$$ACID = \{A, C, I, D\} \tag{31}$$

where: - A represents Atomicity, - C represents Consistency, - I represents Isolation, - D represents Durability.

By breaking down these properties and discussing their implications in real-world scenarios, Stonebraker not only made the material accessible but also inspired students to think critically about the challenges in database management.

Mentorship and Guidance

As a professor, Stonebraker took on the role of mentor, guiding students through their research projects and encouraging them to pursue innovative ideas. He believed that mentorship was crucial in academia, as it helped cultivate the next generation of leaders in the field.

One of his notable protégés, who later became a prominent figure in the database community, credited Stonebraker with instilling a sense of curiosity and a desire for excellence. "He pushed us to think beyond the textbook and to explore the uncharted territories of database technology," the student recalled.

Collaborative Research Initiatives

Stonebraker also emphasized collaboration, often partnering with industry leaders to conduct research that had real-world applications. He initiated projects that involved both students and professionals, creating a symbiotic relationship between academia and industry.

One such project involved the development of a new database management system that utilized a novel architecture for handling large-scale data. This initiative not only provided students with hands-on experience but also resulted in significant contributions to the field.

The collaborative nature of this research was encapsulated in the following equation, representing the synergy between academic research and industry practice:

$$Synergy = \frac{(A + I)}{C} \tag{32}$$

where: - A is the academic contribution, - I is the industrial application, - C is the collaborative effort.

Impact on the Next Generation

Through his teaching and mentorship, Stonebraker left an indelible mark on his students, many of whom went on to make significant contributions to database technology. His influence extended beyond the classroom, as he actively participated in conferences and workshops, sharing his insights and fostering a community of innovation.

In reflecting on his transition to academia, Stonebraker noted, "The satisfaction of seeing my students succeed and innovate is unparalleled. It's a different kind of achievement, one that I cherish deeply." This sentiment encapsulates the essence of his academic journey—a journey that not only transformed his life but also the lives of countless students who were inspired by his passion and expertise.

Conclusion

Transitioning to academia was a pivotal moment in Michael Stonebraker's career. It allowed him to shift from a focus on personal achievements to a commitment to nurturing future talent. His unique blend of industry experience and academic rigor created a rich learning environment that empowered students to push the boundaries of database technology. As he continued to inspire and innovate, Stonebraker solidified his legacy as not only a pioneer in the database field but also as an influential educator shaping the future of computer science.

The Research and Teaching Career: Inspiring the Next Generation

Michael Stonebraker's transition from a pioneering entrepreneur to a trailblazing professor marked a significant chapter in his career, where he not only continued to innovate but also dedicated himself to inspiring the next generation of computer scientists. His teaching philosophy was rooted in the belief that education should be dynamic, engaging, and closely aligned with real-world applications.

Innovative Teaching Methods

Stonebraker employed a variety of innovative teaching methods that challenged traditional pedagogical approaches. He believed in the importance of hands-on learning, which he implemented through project-based assignments that required students to solve real-world database problems. For instance, in his database systems course, students were tasked with developing a mini version of a database management system (DBMS) from scratch. This not only fostered a deeper understanding of database concepts but also encouraged critical thinking and problem-solving skills.

To illustrate the importance of database normalization, he introduced a practical exercise where students had to analyze a poorly designed database schema and apply normalization techniques to improve its structure. The exercise culminated in students presenting their solutions to the class, fostering a collaborative learning environment where peer feedback was encouraged.

Research Contributions

As a researcher, Stonebraker's contributions were instrumental in shaping the curriculum and research focus within the computer science department. He guided students in various research projects that explored cutting-edge topics in database systems, such as distributed databases and big data analytics.

One notable project involved the development of a distributed database system that could efficiently handle large-scale data processing. The research team, under Stonebraker's mentorship, implemented a novel algorithm for data partitioning that significantly improved query performance. The algorithm, denoted as:

$$P(i) = \frac{D(i)}{N} \quad \text{for } i = 1, 2, \ldots, N \tag{33}$$

where $P(i)$ represents the partitioned data for node i, $D(i)$ denotes the original data size for node i, and N is the total number of nodes in the system. This work not only contributed to the academic community but also resulted in several publications in prestigious conferences, further elevating the profile of the university's computer science program.

Mentorship and Guidance

Stonebraker's role as a mentor extended beyond academic instruction; he was deeply invested in the personal and professional development of his students. He organized regular seminars and workshops featuring industry leaders, providing students with invaluable networking opportunities. His encouragement led many students to pursue internships and co-op positions at leading tech companies, where they could apply their classroom knowledge in real-world settings.

One of his former students, Sarah Thompson, credits Stonebraker with igniting her passion for database technologies. "He didn't just teach us how to code; he inspired us to think like innovators," she remarked. Stonebraker's influence extended to guiding students in their career choices, helping them navigate the complexities of the tech industry.

Legacy of Inspiration

The legacy of Michael Stonebraker's teaching career is evident in the success of his students, many of whom have gone on to become leaders in the field of computer science. His commitment to fostering a culture of innovation and inquiry has left an indelible mark on the academic community.

In recognition of his contributions, the university established the "Stonebraker Scholarship," aimed at supporting underrepresented students pursuing degrees in computer science. This initiative reflects his belief in making education accessible to all, ensuring that future generations of computer scientists can benefit from the same opportunities he had.

In conclusion, Michael Stonebraker's research and teaching career exemplifies the profound impact that a dedicated educator can have on the next generation of innovators. Through his innovative teaching methods, commitment to mentorship, and groundbreaking research, he has inspired countless students to push the boundaries of what is possible in the world of databases and beyond. His legacy continues to thrive as his students carry forward his vision of creativity, inquiry, and excellence in the field of computer science.

The Influence on Future Generations: Shaping Minds

Michael Stonebraker's impact on the realm of computer science extends far beyond his groundbreaking innovations in database technology; it encompasses his profound influence on the minds of countless students and emerging professionals in the field. As a trailblazing professor at the University of California, Berkeley, Stonebraker has not only imparted knowledge but has also inspired a generation of thinkers to challenge the status quo and aspire to greatness. This section explores the various dimensions of his influence, the theories he championed, and the legacy he has built through mentorship and teaching.

Theoretical Foundations and Practical Applications

At the core of Stonebraker's teaching philosophy lies a commitment to blending theoretical foundations with practical applications. He often emphasized the importance of understanding the underlying principles of database systems, such as the relational model proposed by E.F. Codd, which serves as the cornerstone of modern databases. The relational model can be succinctly expressed through the following equation:

$$R = \{(a_1, a_2, \ldots, a_n) \mid a_i \in D_i\} \tag{34}$$

where R is a relation, a_i are attributes, and D_i represents the domain of each attribute. Stonebraker encouraged students to grasp the significance of this model, illustrating how it laid the groundwork for innovations like Ingres and Postgres.

In his lectures, Stonebraker often tackled complex problems in database design and management, such as normalization and query optimization. For instance, he would present scenarios where students had to apply normalization forms to eliminate redundancy and ensure data integrity. The normalization process can be summarized by the following series of transformations:

1. **First Normal Form (1NF)**: Ensuring that all attributes are atomic. 2. **Second Normal Form (2NF)**: Removing partial dependencies. 3. **Third Normal Form (3NF)**: Eliminating transitive dependencies.

By engaging students in hands-on projects that required them to implement these concepts, Stonebraker effectively bridged the gap between theory and practice, fostering a deeper understanding of database systems.

Mentorship and Research Opportunities

One of the hallmarks of Stonebraker's influence is his dedication to mentorship. He has played a pivotal role in guiding students through their academic journeys, encouraging them to pursue research opportunities that align with their interests. Many of his students have gone on to make significant contributions to the field, often citing his mentorship as a key factor in their success.

For example, the development of the PostgreSQL database can be traced back to the collaborative efforts of Stonebraker and his students during the late 1980s. This open-source project not only revolutionized the database landscape but also served as a fertile ground for students to engage in real-world problem-solving. The collaborative nature of this project exemplified Stonebraker's belief in the power of teamwork and shared knowledge.

Encouraging Innovation and Critical Thinking

Stonebraker's teaching style is characterized by his encouragement of innovation and critical thinking. He often challenges students to think outside the box and question established norms. This approach is reflected in his own career, where he consistently pushed the boundaries of database technology.

In the classroom, he would present students with case studies of existing database systems, prompting them to identify limitations and propose innovative solutions. For instance, during discussions on the shortcomings of traditional row-based storage, he would introduce the concept of columnar storage, which optimizes read performance for analytical queries. This approach not only stimulated creative thinking but also prepared students to contribute to the evolving landscape of database technologies.

Legacy of Influence

The legacy of Michael Stonebraker's influence is evident in the achievements of his students and the broader database community. Many of his former students have ascended to leadership positions in academia and industry, continuing to propagate the values of innovation, collaboration, and critical inquiry that he instilled in them.

Moreover, Stonebraker's contributions to the field have inspired the establishment of numerous research initiatives and academic programs focused on database technology. Institutions around the world now emphasize the importance of foundational knowledge in database systems, a testament to the enduring impact of his teachings.

In conclusion, Michael Stonebraker's influence on future generations is profound and multifaceted. Through his commitment to education, mentorship, and the promotion of innovative thinking, he has shaped the minds of countless students, empowering them to become the next generation of pioneers in the field of computer science. As they carry forward his legacy, the spirit of inquiry and rebellion that Stonebraker embodies will undoubtedly continue to inspire new breakthroughs in database technology and beyond.

Winning the Turing Award

The Turing Award, often regarded as the "Nobel Prize of Computing," is a prestigious recognition bestowed by the Association for Computing Machinery (ACM) to individuals for their substantial contributions to the computing community. In 2014, Michael Stonebraker was honored with this accolade, a testament to his relentless pursuit of innovation in the field of database systems. This subsection delves into the significance of this award, the contributions that led to this recognition, and the broader implications for the field of computer science.

The Prestigious Recognition: A Testament to Excellence

Winning the Turing Award is not merely an acknowledgment of past achievements; it is a reflection of the recipient's lasting impact on the discipline. The award is named after Alan Turing, a pioneer of theoretical computer science, and it celebrates contributions that have had a profound influence on the computing landscape. Stonebraker's receipt of this honor highlights his role as a catalyst for change in database technology, particularly through his work on relational databases and data management systems.

The Impact of the Turing Award: Paving the Way for Innovations

Stonebraker's work has consistently challenged the status quo in database management. His innovations, particularly in the realm of relational databases, have transformed how data is stored, accessed, and manipulated. The Turing Award citation recognized him specifically for his pioneering work in the development of several influential database systems, including Ingres, Postgres, and more recently, SciDB. Each of these systems introduced groundbreaking concepts that have shaped modern database architectures.

For instance, Postgres introduced the concept of extensibility, allowing users to define their own data types and functions, which was revolutionary at the time. This feature paved the way for more complex data management scenarios, enabling the handling of diverse data types beyond traditional relational models. The introduction of such features exemplifies how Stonebraker's vision has led to significant advancements in database technology.

The Continuing Innovations: A Bright Future Ahead

Receiving the Turing Award also serves as an impetus for further innovation. It not only acknowledges past contributions but also inspires future generations of computer scientists to push boundaries. Stonebraker's recognition has encouraged ongoing research and development in database technologies, leading to new paradigms such as NoSQL databases, cloud-based data storage, and the rise of big data analytics.

In his acceptance speech, Stonebraker emphasized the importance of collaboration and interdisciplinary approaches in advancing technology. He highlighted the need for computer scientists to work closely with domain experts to create systems that are not only technically sound but also practically applicable. This perspective aligns with the evolving nature of data science, where the integration of machine learning, artificial intelligence, and database management is becoming increasingly critical.

Conclusion

Michael Stonebraker's Turing Award is a significant milestone in his illustrious career, underscoring his contributions to the field of computer science and the database community. His work has not only influenced the development of database systems but has also set the stage for future innovations that continue to emerge in this dynamic field. As we look forward to the next generation of database technologies, Stonebraker's legacy serves as a guiding beacon for aspiring computer scientists and innovators, reminding us of the profound impact that one individual's vision can have on the world of technology.

$$\text{Impact} = \sum_{i=1}^{n} \text{Contribution}_i \times \text{Relevance}_i \qquad (35)$$

This equation illustrates the cumulative impact of Stonebraker's contributions, where each contribution is weighted by its relevance to the field. The Turing Award symbolizes the culmination of these efforts, reinforcing the notion that innovation in computer science is both a personal journey and a collective endeavor.

The Prestigious Recognition: A Testament to Excellence

Michael Stonebraker's illustrious career in the realm of databases culminated in a significant milestone: the prestigious Turing Award. This accolade, often referred to as the "Nobel Prize of Computing," is a recognition bestowed by the Association for Computing Machinery (ACM) to individuals for their contributions of lasting importance to computing. Stonebraker received this honor in 2014, an acknowledgment of his pioneering work that has fundamentally shaped the landscape of database systems.

The Significance of the Turing Award

The Turing Award is not merely a trophy; it represents a lifetime of innovation, creativity, and intellectual rigor. The award is given to individuals whose work has had a lasting impact on the computing community. In Stonebraker's case, the award recognized his contributions to the development of relational databases, object-relational databases, and the advancement of data management technologies. The award citation highlighted his role in the creation of Ingres and Postgres, two groundbreaking database systems that introduced concepts still in use today.

Key Contributions Leading to the Award

Stonebraker's journey to the Turing Award was marked by several pivotal contributions that revolutionized the field of database technology:

- **Ingres:** Developed in the 1970s at the University of California, Berkeley, Ingres was one of the first relational database management systems (RDBMS). It introduced the SQL query language, which has become the standard for database queries. The architecture of Ingres paved the way for subsequent database systems and established a foundational framework for relational databases.

- **Postgres:** Following Ingres, Stonebraker led the development of Postgres in the 1980s. This system expanded upon the relational model by introducing object-oriented features, allowing for more complex data types and relationships. Postgres was not just an evolution; it was a revolution in database design, influencing countless systems that followed.

- **Open Source Movement:** Stonebraker was also a strong advocate for open-source software. By releasing Postgres as an open-source project, he democratized access to advanced database technology, enabling developers and organizations worldwide to innovate without the constraints of proprietary software.

- **Column Store Databases:** His work on column-oriented database systems, such as Vertica, further pushed the boundaries of database performance and scalability. These systems are particularly well-suited for analytical workloads, showcasing Stonebraker's ability to foresee the evolving needs of data management.

The Impact of the Turing Award

Receiving the Turing Award not only validated Stonebraker's work but also emphasized the importance of innovation in computer science. The recognition served as a beacon for aspiring computer scientists, illustrating that groundbreaking contributions are possible through dedication and creativity. It also highlighted the significance of collaboration in academia and industry, as many of Stonebraker's achievements were the result of teamwork and shared vision.

Reflections on Excellence

In the years following the award, Stonebraker continued to inspire the next generation of computer scientists. His lectures and mentorship fostered a culture of inquiry and exploration, encouraging students to challenge existing paradigms. His influence extended beyond the classroom, as he became a sought-after speaker at conferences and workshops, sharing insights from his extensive experience.

The Turing Award, therefore, stands as a testament not only to Stonebraker's individual excellence but also to the collaborative spirit that drives innovation in the field of computer science. It serves as a reminder that the pursuit of knowledge and the desire to solve complex problems can lead to extraordinary achievements.

In conclusion, Michael Stonebraker's receipt of the Turing Award encapsulates a career defined by vision, tenacity, and an unwavering commitment to excellence. His work continues to resonate within the database community, influencing new generations of developers and researchers who aspire to leave their mark on the ever-evolving landscape of technology.

The Impact of the Turing Award: Paving the Way for Innovations

The Turing Award, often referred to as the "Nobel Prize of Computing," recognizes individuals for their contributions of lasting importance to computing. Michael Stonebraker's receipt of this prestigious award in 2014 was not merely a personal accolade; it was a significant marker of the transformative impact he had on the field of database systems. This section explores the implications of Stonebraker's Turing Award on the landscape of computer science, particularly in database innovations.

Recognition of Pioneering Work

Stonebraker's Turing Award was awarded for his foundational contributions to the development of relational database systems and his role in advancing database architectures. His work on Ingres and Postgres laid the groundwork for modern database management systems, introducing key concepts such as extensibility and support for complex data types. This recognition served to validate the importance of his innovations, encouraging further research and development in database technologies.

Catalyst for Innovation

The Turing Award often acts as a catalyst for innovation within the field. Stonebraker's recognition inspired a new generation of computer scientists to explore uncharted territories in database technology. His work emphasized the need for systems that could efficiently handle large volumes of data, leading to the emergence of technologies such as NoSQL databases and big data analytics.

$$D = \frac{V}{T} \tag{36}$$

Where D represents data throughput, V is the volume of data processed, and T is the time taken for processing. Stonebraker's influence can be seen in the quest to optimize this equation, pushing the boundaries of how data is managed and analyzed.

Shaping Academic Discourse

Stonebraker's Turing Award also had a profound impact on academic discourse surrounding databases. His recognition brought attention to the importance of database research within computer science curricula. Universities began to prioritize database systems as a critical area of study, leading to the development of specialized programs and courses. This shift in focus produced a wave of research that further explored the scalability, reliability, and performance of database systems.

Influencing Industry Standards

The Turing Award not only influences academia but also the industry. Stonebraker's contributions have shaped industry standards and practices. For instance, the principles established through his work on Postgres have been integrated into many commercial database systems today. This integration has led to improved performance and reliability, setting benchmarks for database technology that companies strive to meet.

Encouraging Open Source Movements

Stonebraker's advocacy for open-source software, particularly with Postgres, has had a lasting impact on the database community. The Turing Award highlighted the significance of open-source projects, encouraging developers to contribute to collaborative efforts. This shift has resulted in a plethora of open-source database solutions, fostering innovation and allowing for rapid advancements in technology.

Legacy of Innovation

The legacy of Stonebraker's Turing Award extends beyond immediate recognition. It serves as a reminder of the potential for innovation in the field of database systems. By paving the way for future developments, Stonebraker's work encourages ongoing exploration of new paradigms in data management. His influence can be seen in current trends such as cloud databases, distributed systems, and machine learning integration within database technologies.

In conclusion, the impact of the Turing Award on Michael Stonebraker's career was profound, serving as a beacon for innovation in database technology. By validating his contributions, the award has inspired further research, shaped academic discourse, influenced industry standards, and encouraged open-source movements. As we look to the future, Stonebraker's legacy continues to pave the way for innovations that will define the next era of database systems.

The Continuing Innovations: A Bright Future Ahead

The landscape of database technology is ever-evolving, and Michael Stonebraker's influence continues to resonate through the corridors of academia and industry alike. His relentless pursuit of innovation has paved the way for groundbreaking advancements, and as we peer into the horizon of database technology, we can identify several key areas where his impact is likely to manifest in the years to come.

Embracing the Era of Big Data

In the age of big data, where organizations are inundated with massive volumes of information, the need for efficient database systems has never been more critical. Stonebraker's contributions to scalable architectures, particularly through systems like *Postgres* and *SciDB*, have laid the groundwork for handling complex datasets. As organizations seek to derive insights from vast amounts of data, the principles of distributed databases and parallel processing will become increasingly relevant.

Consider the following equation, which represents the scalability of a distributed database system:

$$S = \frac{N}{T} \qquad (37)$$

where S is the scalability factor, N is the number of nodes in the system, and T is the time taken to process a query. As N increases, the potential for faster query processing becomes evident, reflecting Stonebraker's vision of harnessing multiple nodes to achieve efficiency.

Advancements in Machine Learning Integration

The integration of machine learning (ML) with database systems is another frontier that promises to redefine data management. Stonebraker's work on *Polystore* exemplifies this trend, allowing users to access data from multiple sources seamlessly. As machine learning algorithms require vast amounts of data for training, the ability to efficiently query and manipulate data from disparate sources will be paramount.

For instance, consider the challenge of querying a heterogeneous data environment, where data is stored in various formats across different systems. A potential solution can be modeled as:

$$Q = \sum_{i=1}^{N} f(D_i) \qquad (38)$$

where Q represents the final query result, D_i denotes the individual data sources, and $f(D_i)$ is the function applied to each data source. This approach reflects the versatility of the Polystore architecture, enabling users to leverage data from SQL databases, NoSQL stores, and file systems in a unified manner.

Fostering a Culture of Open Source Innovation

Stonebraker's advocacy for open source software has significantly influenced the database community. The collaborative nature of open source allows for rapid innovation and adaptation, as developers worldwide contribute to the improvement of existing systems. The ongoing development of projects like *Postgres* and *SciDB* showcases how community-driven efforts can lead to robust and feature-rich database solutions.

As we look ahead, the importance of fostering a culture of open source innovation cannot be overstated. The following equation illustrates the potential growth of an open-source project based on community contributions:

$$G = C \times R \qquad (39)$$

where G is the growth of the project, C represents the number of contributors, and R is the rate of contributions over time. As more developers engage with open-source projects, the potential for rapid advancements in database technologies increases, echoing Stonebraker's vision of collaborative progress.

The Rise of Cloud-Native Databases

With the increasing adoption of cloud computing, the rise of cloud-native databases is inevitable. Stonebraker's foresight into the importance of flexibility and scalability aligns perfectly with the demands of cloud environments. As organizations migrate to the cloud, the need for databases that can seamlessly scale up or down in response to changing workloads will become paramount.

Cloud-native databases leverage microservices architecture and containerization to enhance deployment and management. The following equation can represent the efficiency of resource allocation in a cloud-native environment:

$$E = \frac{R_a}{R_t} \qquad (40)$$

where E is the efficiency of resource allocation, R_a is the allocated resources, and R_t is the total resources required to handle the workload. By optimizing resource allocation, organizations can significantly reduce costs while maintaining high performance, a testament to Stonebraker's enduring legacy of innovation.

Conclusion

As we navigate the uncharted waters of the future, Michael Stonebraker's contributions to the field of databases will undoubtedly continue to inspire and shape the trajectory of technology. His pioneering spirit and unwavering commitment to pushing boundaries will serve as a guiding light for the next generation of innovators. From embracing big data to fostering open-source collaboration and adapting to the cloud-native paradigm, the future of databases is bright, and it is a future that Stonebraker has helped to illuminate.

In the words of Stonebraker himself, "Innovation is not just about new ideas; it's about making those ideas work." With his legacy firmly rooted in the foundation of modern database technology, the journey ahead promises to be filled with exciting challenges and transformative innovations.

The Future Awaits

New Ventures and Innovations

The Invention of SciDB

In the ever-evolving landscape of database technology, Michael Stonebraker's invention of SciDB marked a significant turning point, particularly in the realm of scientific data management. SciDB, short for Scientific Database, was conceived to address the unique challenges posed by the massive datasets generated in various scientific fields, such as genomics, climate modeling, and astrophysics.

The Need for SciDB

As scientific research increasingly relied on large-scale data analysis, traditional relational databases began to show their limitations. These limitations included:

- **Scalability Issues:** Traditional databases struggled to scale horizontally, leading to performance bottlenecks as data volumes grew.

- **Complex Data Types:** Scientific data often involves complex structures (e.g., multi-dimensional arrays) that relational databases are not designed to handle efficiently.

- **Inefficient Querying:** The SQL query language, while powerful for structured data, was not optimized for the types of analytical queries common in scientific research.

To illustrate these challenges, consider a climate model that generates data in the form of a three-dimensional array representing temperature, pressure, and humidity across different geographical locations and time points. Traditional relational databases would require complex joins and transformations to analyze this data, resulting in significant overhead and latency.

The Architecture of SciDB

SciDB was designed with these challenges in mind, introducing a novel architecture that emphasized efficiency and scalability. The core components of SciDB include:

- **Array Data Model:** SciDB utilizes a multi-dimensional array data model, allowing scientists to store and manipulate data in its natural form. This model is particularly suited for scientific applications where data is inherently multi-dimensional.

$$A[i, j, k] = f(x_i, y_j, z_k) \qquad (41)$$

where A represents the array, and f is a function that defines the relationship between the indices i, j, and k.

- **Parallel Processing:** SciDB employs a distributed architecture that supports parallel processing. This allows for efficient data retrieval and computation, leveraging modern multi-core and distributed systems.

- **Flexible Query Language:** SciDB introduced its own query language, AQL (Array Query Language), which is specifically designed for querying multi-dimensional arrays. AQL enables scientists to perform complex analyses without the cumbersome overhead of traditional SQL.

$$\text{SELECT } AVG(A) \text{ FROM } A \text{ WHERE } A[x, y, z] > T \qquad (42)$$

This example demonstrates how AQL can be used to compute the average of an array A where the values exceed a threshold T.

Challenges in Development

The development of SciDB was not without its challenges. Stonebraker and his team faced several hurdles, including:

- **Data Integration:** Integrating diverse scientific datasets from various sources required significant effort to ensure compatibility and usability.

- **User Adoption:** Convincing the scientific community to adopt a new database paradigm posed a challenge, as many researchers were accustomed to traditional relational databases.

- **Performance Optimization:** Fine-tuning the performance of SciDB to handle large-scale datasets efficiently required extensive testing and iteration.

Despite these challenges, the team persevered, driven by the vision of creating a tool that would empower scientists to unlock insights from their data more effectively.

Impact and Applications of SciDB

The introduction of SciDB had a profound impact on the scientific community. It enabled researchers to:

- **Manage Large Datasets:** SciDB allowed for the efficient storage and retrieval of large-scale scientific data, facilitating more complex analyses and experiments.

- **Accelerate Research:** By streamlining data access and analysis, SciDB helped researchers accelerate their work, leading to faster discoveries and innovations.

- **Foster Collaboration:** The open-source nature of SciDB encouraged collaboration among researchers, fostering a community that shared tools and techniques for data analysis.

For instance, in genomics, SciDB has been utilized to analyze large genomic datasets, enabling researchers to identify patterns and correlations that were previously difficult to discern. Similarly, in climate science, SciDB has facilitated the analysis of multi-dimensional climate data, leading to better understanding and modeling of climate change.

Conclusion

In conclusion, the invention of SciDB by Michael Stonebraker represents a pivotal moment in the evolution of databases, particularly for scientific applications. By addressing the unique challenges of managing large, complex datasets, SciDB has transformed how researchers approach data analysis, paving the way for new discoveries and innovations. As the scientific community continues to generate vast amounts of data, the relevance and impact of SciDB are likely to grow, solidifying Stonebraker's legacy as a true pioneer in the field of databases.

The Birth of SciDB: Revolutionizing Scientific Databases

In the early 2000s, the landscape of scientific research was rapidly evolving, characterized by an explosion of data generated from various fields such as genomics, astronomy, and physics. Traditional database systems, designed primarily for transactional data, struggled to accommodate the complex and high-dimensional datasets that scientists were beginning to encounter. Enter Michael Stonebraker, the unfiltered pioneer of databases, who recognized the pressing need for a new kind of database system tailored specifically for scientific applications. This vision culminated in the creation of SciDB.

The Need for a Scientific Database

Scientific data is often multi-dimensional, meaning it can be represented in arrays of various dimensions. For example, a simple two-dimensional array could represent the pixel values of an image, while a three-dimensional array might represent temperature readings across a grid of locations over time. Traditional relational databases, which rely on tables and rows, are ill-suited for such data structures. The challenges included:

- **Performance Issues:** As datasets grew in size and complexity, traditional databases faced significant performance bottlenecks, particularly in terms of query execution time and data retrieval.

- **Data Complexity:** Scientific data often includes not just numerical values, but also metadata, hierarchical relationships, and complex data types that relational databases struggle to represent.

- **Scalability:** The volume of scientific data was increasing exponentially, necessitating a system that could scale horizontally to accommodate this growth.

The Architectural Innovations of SciDB

To address these challenges, SciDB was designed with several key architectural innovations:

- **Array-Based Storage:** Unlike traditional databases, SciDB uses an array-based storage model that allows for the efficient storage and manipulation of multi-dimensional arrays. This model is particularly well-suited for scientific data, enabling operations that are both intuitive and performant.

+ **Built-In Analytics:** SciDB includes a rich set of built-in analytical functions tailored for scientific computing. This allows researchers to perform complex operations directly within the database, reducing the need for external processing and improving overall efficiency.

+ **Parallel Processing:** Leveraging modern multi-core and distributed computing architectures, SciDB supports parallel processing, enabling it to handle large datasets and complex queries with remarkable speed.

+ **Flexible Data Models:** SciDB supports a variety of data types, including arrays, matrices, and tensors, allowing for greater flexibility in how scientists can model and query their data.

Real-World Applications of SciDB

SciDB has found applications across a range of scientific disciplines, showcasing its versatility and effectiveness. Here are a few notable examples:

+ **Genomic Research:** In genomics, researchers often work with vast datasets containing genetic sequences and variations. SciDB enables the efficient storage and querying of these sequences, allowing for rapid analysis and comparison across different samples. For instance, researchers can use SciDB to perform complex queries that identify genetic markers associated with specific diseases.

+ **Environmental Monitoring:** SciDB has been employed in environmental science to manage and analyze data from sensor networks that monitor air and water quality. The ability to handle multi-dimensional time-series data allows scientists to track changes over time and make informed decisions regarding environmental policies.

+ **Astronomy:** In astronomy, large telescopes generate massive amounts of data that need to be processed and analyzed. SciDB's ability to handle high-dimensional data makes it an ideal choice for astronomers, who can store and manipulate data from various celestial observations seamlessly.

Theoretical Underpinnings and Query Language

At the heart of SciDB lies a powerful query language designed specifically for array-based data. This language extends SQL, incorporating array-specific operations such as `ARRAY_AGG`, `ARRAY_JOIN`, and `ARRAY_SLICE`. These functions allow users to perform complex analyses with minimal code, making it accessible to scientists who may not have extensive programming backgrounds.

For example, a typical query in SciDB to calculate the mean of a three-dimensional array of temperature readings might look like this:

```
SELECT AVG(temperature) FROM temperature_data WHERE region = 'Nort
```

This query demonstrates the simplicity and power of SciDB's query language, enabling scientists to derive insights from their data without the overhead of complex programming.

Challenges and Future Directions

While SciDB has made significant strides in revolutionizing scientific databases, it is not without its challenges. The adoption of new technologies often encounters resistance due to established practices and the inertia of legacy systems. Additionally, as scientific data continues to grow in volume and complexity, SciDB must evolve to address new demands, such as real-time data processing and integration with machine learning frameworks.

Looking ahead, the future of SciDB appears promising. With ongoing developments in cloud computing and distributed systems, SciDB is well-positioned to expand its capabilities and reach. The integration of artificial intelligence and machine learning algorithms into its core functionalities could further enhance its analytical capabilities, providing researchers with powerful tools to extract insights from their data.

In conclusion, the birth of SciDB represents a pivotal moment in the evolution of scientific databases. By addressing the unique challenges posed by scientific data and providing innovative solutions, Michael Stonebraker has once again demonstrated his prowess as a pioneer in the field, paving the way for future advancements in data management and analysis.

Unlocking the Potential of SciDB: Pushing Boundaries

SciDB emerged as a groundbreaking solution to the challenges posed by the ever-increasing volume and complexity of scientific data. Traditional database systems often struggled to accommodate the multidimensional nature of scientific data, which is characterized by vast arrays of measurements across multiple dimensions. SciDB was designed specifically to address these needs, pushing the boundaries of what was possible in database management.

Theoretical Foundation

At its core, SciDB is built on the principles of array databases, which treat data as multidimensional arrays rather than traditional tables. This paradigm shift allows for more natural representation and manipulation of scientific datasets. The theoretical foundation of SciDB can be understood through the lens of array algebra, which provides a framework for performing operations on arrays efficiently.

The main operations in array algebra include:

$$\text{Select}(A, \text{condition}) \quad \text{(Filtering rows based on a condition)} \tag{43}$$

$$\text{Project}(A, \text{attributes}) \quad \text{(Selecting specific columns)} \tag{44}$$

$$\text{Join}(A, B) \quad \text{(Combining two arrays based on a key)} \tag{45}$$

$$\text{Aggregate}(A, \text{function}) \quad \text{(Performing calculations across dimensions)} \tag{46}$$

These operations allow researchers to efficiently query and manipulate large datasets, making SciDB an invaluable tool in fields such as genomics, climate modeling, and astrophysics.

Addressing Key Problems

One of the primary problems that SciDB addresses is the challenge of scalability. Traditional relational databases often struggle to manage the sheer volume of data generated by scientific experiments. SciDB employs a distributed architecture, allowing it to scale horizontally across multiple nodes. This design not only enhances performance but also ensures that researchers can work with datasets that would otherwise be unmanageable.

Another significant challenge in scientific computing is the need for complex data analysis. SciDB incorporates advanced analytic functions that enable users to perform sophisticated queries directly within the database. For example, researchers can leverage built-in statistical functions to analyze trends and patterns without the need to export data to external tools.

Real-World Examples

To illustrate the capabilities of SciDB, consider a case study in climate science. Researchers studying climate change often work with vast datasets that include temperature, precipitation, and atmospheric pressure measurements across different geographical locations and time periods. Using SciDB, scientists can perform queries such as:

$$\text{SELECT AVG(Temperature) FROM ClimateData WHERE Year} = 2020 \text{ AND Region} \tag{47}$$

This query allows researchers to quickly compute the average temperature for a specific region and year, demonstrating how SciDB simplifies complex data analysis tasks.

Another example can be found in genomics, where researchers analyze massive datasets of DNA sequences. SciDB's ability to handle multidimensional arrays allows for efficient storage and querying of genetic data. For instance, a query to find the frequency of specific genetic markers across different populations can be executed seamlessly:

$$\text{SELECT COUNT(Marker) FROM GenomicData WHERE Population} = \text{'European'} \tag{48}$$

This capability not only saves time but also enhances the accuracy of genomic studies by allowing for real-time data analysis.

Challenges and Future Directions

Despite its many advantages, SciDB is not without challenges. One of the primary obstacles is the need for specialized knowledge to effectively utilize its features. Researchers must be trained in array database concepts and the specific query language used by SciDB. This learning curve can be a barrier to adoption, particularly in fields where traditional database systems have been the norm.

Moreover, as scientific data continues to grow in complexity, there is an ongoing need for innovations in data management. Future developments in SciDB may focus on enhancing user-friendliness, integrating machine learning capabilities, and improving interoperability with other data analysis tools.

Conclusion

In conclusion, SciDB represents a significant leap forward in the management of scientific data. By unlocking the potential of multidimensional arrays and providing powerful analytic capabilities, it empowers researchers to push the boundaries of discovery. As the landscape of scientific research evolves, SciDB stands poised to play a crucial role in shaping the future of data management, ensuring that researchers can continue to tackle the most pressing challenges of our time.

Challenges Facing SciDB: Overcoming Obstacles

The journey of SciDB, while groundbreaking, has not been without its hurdles. As a pioneering database system designed to handle scientific data, it faced numerous challenges that tested its resilience and adaptability. This section delves into the various obstacles encountered during the development and deployment of SciDB, exploring how they were addressed and the lessons learned in the process.

1. Complexity of Scientific Data

One of the primary challenges SciDB faced was the inherent complexity of scientific data. Unlike traditional databases that often deal with structured data, scientific data is frequently unstructured, high-dimensional, and heterogeneous. This complexity necessitated the development of advanced data models capable of accommodating various data types, such as images, time-series data, and spatial data.

To address this challenge, SciDB implemented a multidimensional array model, allowing users to represent data in a way that reflects its natural structure. The mathematical representation of a multidimensional array can be expressed as:

$$A : \mathbb{R}^{n_1 \times n_2 \times ... \times n_k} \to \mathbb{R} \qquad (49)$$

where A is the array, and $n_1, n_2, \ldots, n_k$ are the dimensions of the data. This approach not only provided flexibility but also facilitated efficient querying and manipulation of complex datasets.

2. Performance and Scalability

As SciDB began to gain traction among researchers, performance and scalability emerged as significant concerns. Scientific datasets can grow exponentially, leading to increased query times and potential bottlenecks in data processing. To tackle these issues, the SciDB team focused on optimizing query execution plans and leveraging parallel processing capabilities.

For instance, they employed a cost-based optimization strategy that analyzed potential execution paths and selected the most efficient one. The optimization process can be mathematically represented as:

$$\text{Cost}(Q) = \sum_{i=1}^{n} w_i \cdot t_i \tag{50}$$

where Q is the query, w_i represents the weight of each operation, and t_i denotes the estimated time for execution. By minimizing the cost function, SciDB could significantly enhance performance and scalability, allowing it to handle larger datasets without compromising speed.

3. User Adoption and Education

Another considerable challenge was user adoption. Many scientists and researchers were accustomed to traditional database systems and were hesitant to transition to a new platform. This reluctance was compounded by the need for education on how to effectively utilize SciDB's unique features.

To facilitate user adoption, the SciDB team developed comprehensive documentation, tutorials, and workshops aimed at educating potential users about the benefits and functionalities of the system. They also engaged with the scientific community through conferences and collaborative projects, showcasing successful case studies that demonstrated SciDB's capabilities.

For example, a collaborative project with a leading research institution illustrated how SciDB could manage and analyze vast amounts of genomic data more efficiently than traditional systems. This real-world application not only showcased SciDB's potential but also helped to build a community of users who could share their experiences and best practices.

4. Integration with Existing Systems

Integrating SciDB with existing data management systems posed another significant obstacle. Many research institutions had established workflows and systems, making it challenging to incorporate a new database without disrupting ongoing projects.

To overcome this barrier, the SciDB team focused on developing robust APIs and connectors that facilitated seamless integration with popular programming languages and data analysis tools, such as Python, R, and MATLAB. This interoperability allowed researchers to leverage SciDB's capabilities while continuing to use their preferred tools.

5. Continuous Development and Support

Finally, the challenge of continuous development and support remained a constant concern. As technology and scientific needs evolved, maintaining and enhancing SciDB required ongoing effort and resources. The team adopted an agile development approach, enabling them to respond quickly to user feedback and emerging trends in scientific research.

Regular updates and community-driven enhancements ensured that SciDB remained relevant and effective in meeting the demands of its users. Moreover, the establishment of a dedicated support forum allowed users to report issues, share solutions, and collaborate on new features, fostering a sense of community around the platform.

In conclusion, while SciDB faced numerous challenges in its quest to revolutionize scientific data management, its innovative approaches to complexity, performance, user education, integration, and continuous improvement have positioned it as a leading solution in the field. The lessons learned from these obstacles not only strengthened SciDB but also paved the way for future innovations in database technology.

The Exploration of Polystore

The concept of Polystore databases emerges as a response to the growing complexity and diversity of data sources in the modern data landscape. Traditional database systems often struggle to efficiently manage and query data spread across heterogeneous sources, which can include relational databases, NoSQL stores, and cloud storage solutions. Polystore aims to unify these disparate data sources under a single query interface, enabling users to seamlessly access and manipulate data regardless of its origin.

1. Definition and Architecture

At its core, a Polystore is defined as a system that integrates multiple data stores, allowing users to query them as if they were a single entity. The architecture of a Polystore typically consists of several key components:

- **Data Sources:** These can include various types of databases such as SQL, NoSQL, graph databases, and even data lakes. Each source retains its original structure and query language.

- **Query Processor:** This component interprets user queries and determines how to distribute them across the various data sources. It translates high-level queries into low-level operations specific to each data store.

- **Data Integration Layer:** This layer is responsible for data transformation and integration, ensuring that data from different sources can be combined and analyzed together.

- **User Interface:** A unified interface that allows users to submit queries and receive results without needing to understand the underlying complexities of each data source.

2. Theoretical Foundations

The theoretical underpinnings of Polystore systems can be traced to several key areas in database research:

2.1. Data Federation Data federation techniques allow for the integration of data from different sources without the need for data replication. This approach is crucial for Polystores, as it enables real-time access to data while maintaining the integrity and performance of the underlying systems.

2.2. Query Optimization Query optimization in a Polystore context involves determining the most efficient way to execute a query across multiple data sources. This requires advanced algorithms that can evaluate the cost of accessing data from different stores, considering factors such as network latency, data size, and the capabilities of each source.

2.3. Schema Mapping Schema mapping is essential in Polystores, as it facilitates the integration of data with varying structures. Techniques such as semantic mapping and schema matching are employed to ensure that data from different sources can be correlated and queried effectively.

3. Challenges and Problems

Despite the potential benefits of Polystore systems, several challenges persist:

3.1. Performance Issues One of the primary concerns with Polystores is performance. The overhead of querying multiple data sources can lead to increased latency, especially if data needs to be transformed or aggregated from various formats.

3.2. Consistency and Integrity Maintaining data consistency across heterogeneous sources is a significant challenge. Different databases may have different update mechanisms, leading to potential data integrity issues.

3.3. Security and Privacy Polystores must also address security concerns, particularly when integrating sensitive data from multiple sources. Ensuring that data access policies are uniformly enforced across all data stores is essential.

4. Real-World Examples

Several real-world implementations of Polystore systems illustrate their effectiveness:

4.1. Google BigQuery Google BigQuery serves as a prime example of a Polystore, allowing users to query data from various sources, including Google Cloud Storage and Google Sheets, using a unified SQL-like interface. Its ability to handle large datasets efficiently showcases the power of Polystore architecture.

4.2. Apache Drill Apache Drill is an open-source Polystore that enables users to query data from different sources, including HDFS, NoSQL databases, and even traditional relational databases. Its schema-free JSON model allows for flexible querying across diverse data formats.

4.3. IBM Watson IBM Watson employs a Polystore approach to integrate data from various healthcare databases, enabling comprehensive analysis and insights. By leveraging multiple data sources, Watson can provide more accurate recommendations and predictions in the medical field.

5. Future Directions

The exploration of Polystore systems is still in its infancy, and several future directions warrant attention:

5.1. Enhanced Query Optimization Techniques As data sources continue to grow in number and complexity, developing more sophisticated query optimization algorithms will be crucial for improving performance.

5.2. Machine Learning Integration Integrating machine learning capabilities into Polystore systems could enhance data analysis, allowing for predictive analytics and automated decision-making based on integrated data sources.

5.3. Standardization Efforts Efforts to establish standards for Polystore architectures and query languages could facilitate broader adoption and interoperability among different systems.

In conclusion, the exploration of Polystore databases represents a significant advancement in the field of data management. By addressing the challenges of integrating diverse data sources, Polystores have the potential to transform how organizations access and utilize their data, paving the way for innovative applications and insights.

Introducing Polystore: A Multi-Dimensional Approach

In the ever-evolving landscape of data management, the emergence of Polystore systems marks a significant shift in how we approach the storage and retrieval of diverse data types. Unlike traditional database systems that typically focus on a single data model, Polystore systems are designed to integrate multiple data models and storage technologies into a unified framework. This multi-dimensional approach allows for greater flexibility, efficiency, and performance in handling complex data requirements.

The Need for Polystore Systems

As organizations increasingly rely on a variety of data sources, including structured, semi-structured, and unstructured data, the limitations of monolithic databases become apparent. Traditional relational database management systems (RDBMS) excel in handling structured data but struggle with the complexities of unstructured data, such as text documents, images, and social media feeds. Furthermore, the rise of big data technologies, such as NoSQL databases, has introduced new challenges in data integration and management.

Polystore systems address these challenges by enabling seamless access to multiple data stores, each optimized for specific data types and access patterns. This flexibility allows organizations to leverage the strengths of various storage

NEW VENTURES AND INNOVATIONS

technologies while minimizing the overhead associated with data movement and transformation.

Architectural Overview

At its core, a Polystore system consists of several key components:

- **Data Sources:** Various databases and data stores, including SQL databases, NoSQL databases, data lakes, and file systems, serve as the underlying data sources.

- **Data Integration Layer:** This layer is responsible for querying and integrating data from multiple sources. It abstracts the complexity of dealing with different data models and provides a unified query interface.

- **Query Processing Engine:** The engine optimizes and executes queries across heterogeneous data sources, ensuring efficient data retrieval and processing.

- **User Interface:** A user-friendly interface allows users to interact with the Polystore system, enabling them to formulate queries and visualize results without needing in-depth knowledge of the underlying data stores.

Query Language and Processing

Polystore systems typically utilize a unified query language that extends traditional SQL to accommodate various data models. This language allows users to write queries that can span multiple data sources, leveraging the strengths of each system. For example, a user might want to join data from a relational database with information from a document store, which can be expressed in a Polystore query as follows:

$$\text{SELECT } a.name, b.content \text{ FROM RelationalDB}.a \text{ JOIN DocumentStore}.b \text{ ON } a.id \tag{51}$$

This query illustrates the power of Polystore systems in enabling complex data interactions across disparate sources, all while maintaining a coherent syntax that is familiar to SQL users.

Challenges and Considerations

Despite their advantages, Polystore systems face several challenges that must be addressed to ensure their success:

- **Data Consistency:** Maintaining data consistency across different data sources can be challenging, particularly in scenarios involving concurrent updates. Strategies such as eventual consistency and conflict resolution must be implemented to address these issues.

- **Performance Optimization:** Query performance can vary significantly depending on the underlying data sources and their respective architectures. Optimizing queries for heterogeneous environments requires sophisticated query planning and execution strategies.

- **Security and Access Control:** Ensuring secure access to multiple data sources necessitates robust authentication and authorization mechanisms. A comprehensive security model must be established to protect sensitive data across the Polystore environment.

Real-World Applications

Polystore systems have found applications in various domains, demonstrating their versatility and effectiveness. For instance:

- **E-Commerce:** Online retailers leverage Polystore architectures to integrate customer data from relational databases, product information from NoSQL stores, and user-generated content from social media platforms. This holistic view allows for enhanced customer insights and personalized marketing strategies.

- **Healthcare:** In healthcare, Polystore systems enable the integration of clinical data from electronic health records (EHRs), imaging data from PACS systems, and genomic data from research databases. This comprehensive data integration supports advanced analytics and improves patient outcomes.

- **Smart Cities:** Smart city initiatives utilize Polystore systems to aggregate data from various sensors, social media feeds, and public databases. This integrated approach facilitates real-time decision-making and enhances urban planning efforts.

Future Directions

As the demand for diverse data integration continues to grow, the future of Polystore systems looks promising. Innovations in data processing technologies, such as machine learning and artificial intelligence, will further enhance the capabilities of Polystore architectures. Additionally, the ongoing evolution of cloud computing and serverless architectures will provide new opportunities for deploying Polystore systems at scale.

In conclusion, Polystore systems represent a transformative approach to data management, enabling organizations to navigate the complexities of multi-dimensional data landscapes. By integrating various data models and storage technologies, Polystore systems empower users to extract valuable insights from diverse data sources while overcoming the limitations of traditional database systems.

The Applications of Polystore: Endless Possibilities

The advent of Polystore databases has opened up a myriad of applications across various domains, showcasing the versatility and power of this innovative approach to data management. Polystore systems allow for the integration of multiple data models, enabling organizations to leverage the strengths of each model while addressing specific use cases. This section delves into the diverse applications of Polystore databases, highlighting their potential to revolutionize data handling in several key areas.

1. Data Integration and Analytics

One of the most compelling applications of Polystore databases is in the realm of data integration and analytics. Traditional databases often struggle with the challenge of integrating disparate data sources, leading to inefficiencies and data silos. Polystore systems, however, are designed to seamlessly connect various data models, allowing organizations to conduct comprehensive analyses across different data types.

For instance, consider a retail company that collects data from multiple sources: transactional data from a relational database, customer interaction data from a NoSQL document store, and social media sentiment data from a graph database. A Polystore architecture can enable analysts to query and analyze this data in a unified manner, providing insights that would be difficult to achieve with a traditional database system.

The ability to perform complex queries across multiple data models can be mathematically represented as follows:

$$Q_{\text{polystore}}(D_1, D_2, \ldots, D_n) = \bigcup_{i=1}^{n} Q_i(D_i) \qquad (52)$$

where $Q_{\text{polystore}}$ represents the query executed across the Polystore, D_i denotes the individual data sources, and Q_i is the query applied to each data source.

2. Enhanced Decision-Making

Polystore databases facilitate enhanced decision-making by providing a more holistic view of organizational data. By integrating structured, semi-structured, and unstructured data, decision-makers can access a comprehensive dataset that reflects the multifaceted nature of their business environment.

For example, a healthcare organization might utilize a Polystore to aggregate patient records (stored in a relational database), medical imaging data (stored in a binary large object storage), and research publications (stored in a document database). This integrated approach allows healthcare professionals to make informed decisions based on a complete understanding of patient history, treatment outcomes, and the latest research findings.

The decision-making process can be modeled as follows:

$$D_{\text{decision}} = f(Q_{\text{polystore}}(D_1, D_2, D_3)) \qquad (53)$$

where D_{decision} represents the outcome of the decision-making process, and f is a function that encapsulates the logic of decision-making based on integrated data.

3. Real-Time Data Processing

In an era where real-time data processing is paramount, Polystore databases excel by providing the ability to handle streaming data alongside historical data. This capability is particularly beneficial in industries such as finance, telecommunications, and IoT, where timely insights can lead to competitive advantages.

For instance, a telecommunications company can utilize a Polystore to analyze call data records (CDRs) in real-time from a time-series database, while simultaneously referencing customer profiles stored in a relational database. This enables the company to detect anomalies, such as unusual calling patterns, and respond promptly to potential fraud.

The real-time processing capability can be expressed as:

$$T_{\text{response}} = \Delta t(Q_{\text{polystore}}(D_{\text{stream}}, D_{\text{historical}})) \qquad (54)$$

where $T_{response}$ is the time taken to respond to an event, Δt is the time interval for processing, and D_{stream} and $D_{historical}$ represent streaming and historical data, respectively.

4. Support for Diverse Applications

Polystore databases support a wide range of applications across various industries, including:

- **E-commerce:** By integrating product catalogs, customer reviews, and social media interactions, Polystore systems can enhance personalized shopping experiences and optimize inventory management.

- **Finance:** Financial institutions can leverage Polystore databases to analyze transactional data, market trends, and customer behavior, enabling them to develop better risk management strategies and investment decisions.

- **Smart Cities:** Polystore architectures can facilitate the integration of data from sensors, traffic systems, and public services, allowing city planners to optimize resource allocation and improve urban living conditions.

5. Conclusion

In conclusion, the applications of Polystore databases are as diverse as the data they manage. By enabling seamless integration across various data models, Polystore systems empower organizations to unlock insights, enhance decision-making, and respond to real-time challenges. As we continue to generate and consume data at an unprecedented rate, the importance of Polystore databases in shaping the future of data management cannot be overstated. The possibilities are indeed endless, and as Michael Stonebraker's legacy continues to inspire innovations, the potential of Polystore databases will undoubtedly expand, paving the way for new frontiers in data science and analytics.

The Future of Polystore: Opening Doors to Innovation

The Polystore database architecture represents a significant leap forward in the evolution of data management systems. As we delve into the future of Polystore, it becomes crucial to explore its potential to revolutionize how data is stored, queried, and analyzed across multiple data models. This section will examine the theoretical underpinnings of Polystore, the challenges it seeks to address, and the innovative applications that are likely to emerge as this technology matures.

Theoretical Foundations of Polystore

At its core, a Polystore system integrates various data storage technologies, allowing users to manage diverse data formats and models seamlessly. The theoretical framework for Polystore can be described using the following concepts:

- **Data Heterogeneity:** Polystore systems embrace the heterogeneity of data by supporting multiple data models, such as relational, NoSQL, and graph databases. This flexibility allows organizations to use the best storage solution for each data type while maintaining a unified access layer.

- **Data Federation:** Polystore architecture employs data federation techniques, enabling users to query data across different stores without needing to move or replicate it. This is often achieved through a middleware layer that translates queries into the appropriate language for each underlying data source.

- **Query Optimization:** A critical component of Polystore systems is the ability to optimize queries across multiple data sources. This involves selecting the most efficient execution plan based on the data distribution, query complexity, and available resources.

The mathematical representation of query optimization in a Polystore can be expressed as:

$$Q_{opt} = \arg\min_{Q \in Q_{possible}} \text{Cost}(Q) \tag{55}$$

where Q_{opt} is the optimal query, $Q_{possible}$ is the set of all possible queries, and $\text{Cost}(Q)$ represents the estimated execution cost of each query.

Addressing Current Challenges

Despite its promise, the future of Polystore is not without challenges. As organizations increasingly rely on diverse data sources, they encounter several issues that Polystore aims to address:

- **Data Silos:** Organizations often face challenges due to data being stored in isolated systems, leading to inefficiencies and incomplete insights. Polystore aims to break down these silos by providing a unified interface for accessing disparate data sources.

- **Complexity of Data Management:** Managing multiple databases can be cumbersome, with each system requiring different maintenance and operational procedures. Polystore simplifies this complexity by allowing organizations to operate under a single management paradigm.

- **Scalability and Performance:** As data volumes grow, traditional databases struggle to maintain performance. Polystore's architecture is designed to scale horizontally, distributing workloads across multiple data stores to enhance performance.

Innovative Applications of Polystore

The versatility of Polystore opens the door to numerous innovative applications across various industries. Some notable examples include:

- **Healthcare Analytics:** In the healthcare sector, Polystore can integrate electronic health records, genomic data, and clinical trial information. This unified approach enables healthcare providers to perform comprehensive analyses, leading to improved patient outcomes.

- **Financial Services:** Financial institutions can leverage Polystore to combine transactional data, market data, and customer information. This integration facilitates real-time fraud detection and enhances customer relationship management.

- **Smart Cities:** Polystore can play a crucial role in the development of smart cities by aggregating data from various sources, such as IoT devices, traffic management systems, and environmental sensors. This holistic view enables city planners to make data-driven decisions for urban development.

Future Directions and Research Opportunities

As Polystore technology continues to evolve, several research opportunities emerge:

- **Advanced Query Languages:** Developing new query languages that can efficiently handle multi-model queries across diverse data sources is a critical area of research. These languages must balance expressiveness with performance.

- **Security and Privacy:** With the integration of various data sources, ensuring data security and privacy becomes paramount. Research into robust security models that can operate across heterogeneous systems will be essential.

- **Machine Learning Integration:** Integrating machine learning capabilities into Polystore systems can enhance data analysis and decision-making processes. Research can focus on how to best leverage machine learning algorithms to process and analyze data stored in a Polystore.

In conclusion, the future of Polystore is bright, with immense potential to unlock new avenues of innovation across industries. By addressing current challenges and embracing the diverse nature of data, Polystore systems are poised to become a cornerstone of modern data management strategies. As researchers and practitioners continue to explore this exciting landscape, we can anticipate groundbreaking advancements that will shape the future of data-driven decision-making.

The Legacy and Impact

Stonebraker's Influence on the Database Industry

Michael Stonebraker's impact on the database industry is akin to that of a master architect reshaping the skyline of a city; his innovations have not only transformed existing structures but have also paved the way for entirely new paradigms. His work has introduced concepts that have become foundational to modern database systems, influencing both academic research and commercial applications.

At the heart of Stonebraker's influence lies his pioneering work on relational databases, particularly through the development of **Ingres** and **Postgres**. Ingres, developed during the 1970s at the University of California, Berkeley, was one of the first implementations of the relational model proposed by E.F. Codd. The introduction of SQL (Structured Query Language) as a standard interface for database interaction can be traced back to this seminal project. Stonebraker's insistence on rigorous theoretical foundations enabled Ingres to challenge existing hierarchical and network database models, leading to a paradigm shift in how data was stored and accessed.

$$R = \{(a_1, b_1), (a_2, b_2), \ldots, (a_n, b_n)\} \tag{56}$$

where R is a relation, and each tuple represents a record in the database. This mathematical representation of data laid the groundwork for subsequent database designs and implementations.

Following Ingres, Stonebraker's work on **Postgres** in the late 1980s further expanded the capabilities of relational databases by introducing advanced features

THE LEGACY AND IMPACT

such as support for complex data types, object-oriented programming concepts, and extensibility through user-defined types and functions. This innovation was crucial in addressing the limitations of traditional relational databases, particularly in handling complex data structures common in applications like Geographic Information Systems (GIS) and multimedia databases.

The significance of Postgres is encapsulated in its ability to support a wide range of data models, including:

- Relational
- Object-relational
- Document-oriented

This versatility has positioned Postgres as a leading choice for developers seeking a robust, flexible database solution capable of adapting to evolving data requirements.

Stonebraker's influence extends beyond specific technologies; he has been a vocal advocate for the **open-source movement.** By promoting the idea that software should be freely available and modifiable, he has inspired a generation of developers to contribute to and innovate within the database ecosystem. The open-source nature of Postgres has fostered a vibrant community, leading to enhancements and widespread adoption across various industries.

Moreover, Stonebraker's insights into the limitations of traditional database systems have spurred the development of new architectures. His work on **column-oriented databases** through projects like **Mondrian** has revolutionized data warehousing and analytical processing. The columnar storage model, which stores data in columns rather than rows, significantly improves query performance for read-heavy workloads, particularly in big data scenarios. This shift is mathematically represented as:

$$\text{Performance Gain} = \frac{\text{Query Time (Row-oriented)}}{\text{Query Time (Column-oriented)}} \qquad (57)$$

where a lower query time indicates a more efficient database system.

The legacy of Stonebraker's contributions is evident in the proliferation of modern databases that adopt his principles. Technologies such as Apache Cassandra, Google Bigtable, and Amazon Redshift owe their design philosophies to the foundational work laid by Stonebraker. His relentless pursuit of innovation and improvement has not only shaped the database landscape but has also encouraged a culture of experimentation and disruption within the industry.

In summary, Michael Stonebraker's influence on the database industry is profound and multifaceted. From his groundbreaking work on Ingres and Postgres to his advocacy for open-source principles and the development of new database architectures, Stonebraker has left an indelible mark on the field. His contributions continue to inspire future generations of database professionals and researchers, ensuring that his legacy will endure for years to come.

A Pioneering Spirit: Transforming the Landscape

Michael Stonebraker's contributions to the field of databases have not only been groundbreaking but have also fundamentally transformed the landscape of data management. His pioneering spirit is reflected in his relentless pursuit of innovation, challenging established norms, and advocating for new paradigms that have shaped the way we interact with data today.

Redefining Data Management

At the heart of Stonebraker's legacy is his ability to redefine data management through the introduction of novel concepts and technologies. One of his most significant contributions is the concept of the relational database model, which emerged from his work on Ingres. The relational model introduced a systematic way to manage and query data using structured query language (SQL), which has become the backbone of modern database systems.

The relational model can be mathematically represented as follows:

$$R = \{(a_1, a_2, ..., a_n) | a_i \in A_i \text{ for } i = 1, 2, ..., n\} \tag{58}$$

where R is a relation, a_i are attributes, and A_i are the domains of those attributes. This formalism allows for a clear understanding of how data can be structured and manipulated, leading to more efficient data retrieval and management.

Challenging the Status Quo

Stonebraker's work has consistently challenged the status quo in database technology. His creation of Postgres further exemplified this spirit of innovation. Postgres introduced advanced features such as support for complex data types, rules, and triggers, which allowed for greater flexibility in handling diverse data workloads. For instance, the ability to define custom data types enabled users to

THE LEGACY AND IMPACT 113

tailor the database to specific application needs, thus enhancing performance and usability.

The introduction of the object-relational model in Postgres can be expressed as:

$$ORDB = R \cup O \qquad (59)$$

where $ORDB$ represents an object-relational database that combines traditional relational structures R with object-oriented features O. This synthesis allowed for the modeling of real-world entities more naturally, providing a powerful tool for developers and data scientists alike.

Innovations in Performance and Scalability

Stonebraker's innovations did not stop at data modeling; he also focused on performance and scalability. The development of column-oriented databases, such as those pioneered by his work on Mondrian, revolutionized how data is stored and accessed, particularly for analytical workloads. Unlike traditional row-oriented databases, column stores optimize data retrieval by storing data in columns rather than rows, which significantly enhances query performance for read-heavy operations.

The performance improvement can be mathematically represented by the reduction in I/O operations required for queries:

$$I/O_{column} < I/O_{row} \qquad (60)$$

where I/O_{column} denotes the input/output operations for a column store and I/O_{row} for a row store. This efficiency is particularly beneficial in scenarios involving large datasets and complex queries, making column stores a preferred choice for data warehousing applications.

The Open Source Movement and Its Implications

Another transformative aspect of Stonebraker's work is his advocacy for the open-source movement in database technology. By making systems like Postgres freely available, he democratized access to powerful data management tools, enabling a broader range of users—from startups to large enterprises—to leverage cutting-edge technology without the prohibitive costs associated with proprietary solutions.

The implications of this shift are profound. Open-source databases have fostered a collaborative environment where developers can contribute to the evolution of the technology, leading to rapid advancements and a rich ecosystem of extensions and tools. This community-driven approach has resulted in increased innovation and resilience in the database landscape.

Legacy of a Transformative Figure

Stonebraker's pioneering spirit is evident not only in his technical contributions but also in his influence on the next generation of database researchers and practitioners. His role as a professor and mentor has inspired countless individuals to pursue careers in data science and database engineering, ensuring that his legacy continues to shape the future of the industry.

In summary, Michael Stonebraker's impact on the database landscape is nothing short of revolutionary. Through his innovative approaches to data management, challenge to established norms, and commitment to open-source principles, he has transformed the way we think about and interact with data. His work serves as a testament to the power of a pioneering spirit in driving progress and innovation in technology.

Paradigm Shifts: Challenging the Status Quo

Michael Stonebraker's journey through the realm of databases is not merely a tale of technological advancements; it is a narrative punctuated by bold paradigm shifts that have consistently challenged the status quo. His pioneering spirit has led to transformative changes that have redefined how data is stored, accessed, and analyzed. This section delves into these paradigm shifts, examining their theoretical underpinnings, the problems they addressed, and the profound implications they have had on the database industry.

Theoretical Foundations of Paradigm Shifts

At the heart of any paradigm shift lies a fundamental theory that questions existing beliefs and practices. Thomas Kuhn, in his seminal work *The Structure of Scientific Revolutions*, posits that scientific progress occurs not through a linear accumulation of knowledge but through revolutionary changes in the underlying frameworks that govern scientific thought. Stonebraker's contributions exemplify Kuhn's theory, as he consistently challenged established norms and introduced innovative concepts that reshaped the database landscape.

For instance, the development of the relational database model by Edgar F. Codd in the 1970s was a paradigm shift that moved away from hierarchical and network models. This model introduced the concept of data being organized in tables, which

THE LEGACY AND IMPACT   115

allowed for greater flexibility and ease of use. Stonebraker's work with Ingres and Postgres built upon this foundation, pushing the boundaries further by integrating advanced features such as object-relational capabilities and support for complex data types.

Addressing Existing Problems

One of the key drivers of Stonebraker's paradigm shifts has been the need to address existing problems within the database ecosystem. Traditional relational databases, while revolutionary, faced limitations in scalability, performance, and the ability to handle diverse data types. As data volumes exploded in the 1990s and 2000s, the inadequacies of these systems became increasingly apparent.

Stonebraker's response to these challenges was to advocate for new database architectures that could accommodate the evolving needs of users. For example, the introduction of column-oriented storage with systems like Mondrian addressed performance issues associated with analytical queries. By storing data in columns rather than rows, Mondrian optimized read operations, significantly improving query performance for data warehousing applications.

Examples of Paradigm Shifts

Several notable examples illustrate how Stonebraker's innovations have led to paradigm shifts within the database industry:

- **From Row-Based to Column-Based Storage:** The emergence of columnar databases, such as those inspired by Mondrian, marked a significant shift in how data was organized and accessed. Traditional row-based storage was ill-suited for analytical workloads, where queries often required accessing only a subset of columns. Columnar storage allowed for faster data retrieval and reduced I/O operations, leading to enhanced performance in data analytics.

- **The Rise of Open Source Movement:** Stonebraker's advocacy for open-source projects, particularly with Postgres, challenged the proprietary nature of database systems. By making powerful database technology accessible to a broader audience, he democratized data management and encouraged community-driven innovation. This shift has led to the proliferation of open-source databases that rival their commercial counterparts in performance and features.

- **Introduction of New Data Models:** The advent of NoSQL databases, such as MongoDB and Cassandra, represents another paradigm shift that

Stonebraker's work helped catalyze. As applications demanded greater flexibility and scalability, traditional relational models struggled to keep pace. NoSQL databases introduced new data models—document, key-value, and wide-column stores—that allowed for dynamic schema designs and horizontal scaling. Stonebraker's insights into data management paved the way for these innovations, which have become integral to modern application development.

- **Emphasis on Real-Time Data Processing:** The shift towards real-time analytics and data processing has also been influenced by Stonebraker's work. With the rise of big data technologies like Apache Kafka and Apache Spark, the demand for systems capable of processing streams of data in real time has surged. Stonebraker's emphasis on performance and efficiency has informed the development of these technologies, enabling organizations to derive insights from data as it is generated.

Implications of Paradigm Shifts

The implications of these paradigm shifts are profound and far-reaching. They have not only transformed the technical landscape of databases but have also influenced organizational strategies and practices. Companies that have embraced these shifts have gained competitive advantages by leveraging data more effectively, driving innovation, and enhancing decision-making processes.

Moreover, Stonebraker's legacy extends beyond technology; it encompasses a cultural shift within the database community. By challenging the status quo, he has inspired a generation of database professionals to think critically about existing systems and to pursue innovative solutions. This spirit of inquiry and rebellion against complacency is vital for the continued evolution of the database industry.

In conclusion, Michael Stonebraker's contributions to the database field exemplify the power of paradigm shifts in challenging the status quo. His work has not only addressed critical problems within the industry but has also laid the groundwork for future innovations. As we look ahead, the legacy of these shifts will continue to shape the trajectory of database technology, ensuring that it remains responsive to the ever-changing needs of users and organizations alike.

Reflections on Stonebraker's Contributions: Leaving a Lasting Mark

Michael Stonebraker stands as a colossus in the realm of database technology, his contributions reverberating through the industry like the ripples of a stone cast into a still pond. His work has not only transformed how we store and manage data but has also influenced the very paradigms upon which modern computing rests. In this section, we reflect on the remarkable legacy of Stonebraker, highlighting key contributions that have left an indelible mark on the database landscape.

Challenging Conventional Wisdom

At the heart of Stonebraker's influence is his relentless challenge to conventional wisdom. He recognized early on that the relational model, while revolutionary, had its limitations. This insight led to the development of systems like Ingres and Postgres, which introduced concepts such as object-relational databases and extensibility. Stonebraker's willingness to question the status quo is encapsulated in his assertion, "The best way to predict the future is to invent it." This philosophy not only inspired innovation but also encouraged a culture of experimentation in database research.

The Impact of Ingres and Postgres

Ingres, developed in the 1970s, was a pioneering effort that demonstrated the practical application of the relational model. It provided a robust framework for querying data using SQL, which has become the de facto standard for database interaction. The introduction of Postgres in the 1980s pushed the boundaries even further by incorporating features such as complex data types and user-defined functions. These innovations addressed the shortcomings of traditional relational databases, allowing for greater flexibility in handling diverse data types and structures.

The significance of these contributions can be illustrated through the equation representing the relational model:

$$R = \{(a_1, a_2, \ldots, a_n) \mid a_i \in D_i \text{ for } i = 1, 2, \ldots, n\} \tag{61}$$

where R is a relation defined by tuples a_i drawn from distinct domains D_i. This foundational concept laid the groundwork for the development of more complex database systems, influencing generations of database designers and users.

Innovations in Data Management

Stonebraker's work extended beyond relational databases. His involvement in the development of Illustra introduced the concept of object-relational databases, which merged the benefits of object-oriented programming with relational database management. This innovation addressed the growing need for more sophisticated data management solutions, particularly in applications involving complex data types such as multimedia and spatial data.

Moreover, his contributions to the design of columnar databases, exemplified by Mondrian, revolutionized data storage and retrieval. Column stores allow for efficient data compression and faster query performance, particularly for analytical workloads. The equation for a columnar storage model can be represented as:

$$\text{Column Store} = \{C_1, C_2, \ldots, C_m\} \tag{62}$$

where each C_i represents a column of data, enabling efficient access patterns that differ from traditional row-oriented databases. This approach has reshaped data warehousing and analytics, providing the backbone for modern big data applications.

Academic Influence and Mentorship

Beyond his technical contributions, Stonebraker's impact as an educator and mentor cannot be overstated. His tenure at the University of California, Berkeley, produced a generation of database researchers who have gone on to make significant contributions in their own right. Stonebraker's ability to inspire students is reflected in his teaching philosophy, which emphasizes the importance of hands-on experience and real-world applications of theoretical concepts.

The legacy of his mentorship is evident in the accolades received by his students, many of whom have been recognized with prestigious awards, including the ACM SIGMOD Edgar F. Codd Innovations Award. This cycle of knowledge transfer not only perpetuates Stonebraker's influence but also ensures that the field of database research continues to evolve and thrive.

A Lasting Legacy

In conclusion, Michael Stonebraker's contributions to the field of databases have left a lasting mark that transcends individual technologies. His pioneering spirit and willingness to embrace change have fostered an environment of innovation that continues to challenge and expand the boundaries of what is possible in data management. As we look to the future, the principles and systems he championed will undoubtedly serve as a foundation for the next generation of database technologies, ensuring that his impact will be felt for decades to come.

In reflecting on Stonebraker's journey, we are reminded of the words of the great philosopher Aristotle: "The roots of education are bitter, but the fruit is sweet." Stonebraker's path, marked by challenges and triumphs, embodies this

THE LEGACY AND IMPACT

sentiment, leaving an enduring legacy that inspires all who dare to dream and innovate in the world of databases.

The Unfiltered Pioneer

Michael Stonebraker is often described as an unfiltered pioneer in the field of databases, a title that captures his audacious approach to innovation and his relentless pursuit of excellence. This section explores the essence of his pioneering spirit, his willingness to challenge established norms, and the profound impact he has had on the database industry.

The Essence of the Unfiltered Pioneer

At the core of Stonebraker's approach lies an unyielding commitment to questioning the status quo. His career has been characterized by a series of bold moves that often defied conventional wisdom. For instance, while many of his contemporaries adhered to traditional relational database models, Stonebraker ventured into uncharted territories, advocating for new paradigms such as object-relational databases and columnar storage.

Stonebraker's philosophy can be encapsulated in the following equation, which reflects his belief in innovation through disruption:

$$I = D + E \tag{63}$$

Where:

- I represents innovation,
- D denotes disruption of existing norms, and
- E signifies the exploration of new ideas.

This equation highlights that true innovation often arises from a combination of challenging existing frameworks and the courage to explore new concepts.

Challenging Established Norms

One of Stonebraker's most significant contributions to the database landscape is his role in the development of Ingres and Postgres at the University of California, Berkeley. Ingres was revolutionary, as it was one of the first databases to implement the relational model proposed by E.F. Codd. However, Stonebraker did not stop there; he recognized the limitations of traditional relational databases and sought to address them with Postgres.

Postgres introduced several groundbreaking features, such as:

- Support for complex data types,

- Object-oriented capabilities, and

- Advanced indexing techniques.

These innovations were not merely incremental improvements; they represented a paradigm shift that challenged the very foundations of database design. Stonebraker's willingness to push the boundaries of what a database could be set the stage for future advancements in the field.

The Legacy of Disruption

The impact of Stonebraker's pioneering spirit is evident in the numerous projects and companies he has influenced throughout his career. His work on Illustra, for example, introduced revolutionary features that redefined how databases could handle complex data types and multimedia content. Illustra's innovations paved the way for the emergence of object-relational databases, which are now widely used in various applications.

Moreover, Stonebraker's creation of column-store databases, exemplified by his work on Mondrian, revolutionized data storage and retrieval. Column-stores optimize the way data is organized, allowing for faster query performance and improved compression rates. This innovation has been particularly impactful in the era of big data, where the ability to efficiently process vast amounts of information is paramount.

Real-World Applications and Challenges

The principles championed by Stonebraker are not just theoretical; they have real-world applications that address contemporary challenges in data management. For instance, the rise of data analytics and machine learning has necessitated new approaches to data storage and retrieval. Stonebraker's work on SciDB, which focuses on scientific data management, exemplifies how his pioneering spirit continues to drive innovation in response to evolving needs.

However, the journey of an unfiltered pioneer is not without its challenges. For every success, there are lessons learned from failures. The rise and fall of Illustra

THE LEGACY AND IMPACT 121

serve as a poignant reminder that even groundbreaking innovations can face hurdles in the marketplace. The acquisition of Illustra by Informix, while initially promising, ultimately led to a series of challenges that highlighted the complexities of integrating innovative technologies into established companies.

Reflections on Stonebraker's Contributions

In reflecting on Michael Stonebraker's contributions to the database industry, it is clear that his unfiltered approach has left an indelible mark. He has not only transformed the landscape of database technology but has also inspired a new generation of innovators to challenge existing paradigms. His legacy is characterized by a spirit of inquiry and a willingness to embrace risk, traits that are essential for any pioneer.

As we look to the future, the principles embodied by Stonebraker will undoubtedly continue to shape the evolution of database technologies. The ongoing exploration of new architectures, such as Polystore, demonstrates that the quest for innovation is far from over. Stonebraker's influence serves as a guiding light for those who dare to dream and disrupt.

In conclusion, Michael Stonebraker stands as a testament to the power of being an unfiltered pioneer. His contributions have not only advanced the field of databases but have also challenged us to think critically about the future of technology. As we navigate the complexities of a data-driven world, the lessons learned from Stonebraker's journey will continue to inspire and inform the next generation of innovators.

Index

-effectiveness, 24

a, 1–13, 15, 17–20, 22–50, 52–76, 78–87, 89–103, 105–108, 110, 111, 113, 114, 116–119, 121
ability, 2, 10, 12, 27–30, 37, 40, 51, 54, 59–62, 66, 69, 96, 101, 105, 106, 111, 112, 115, 120
academia, 3, 69, 70, 72–75, 82, 84, 85
acceptance, 80
access, 9, 10, 12, 21, 27, 30, 48, 50, 67, 99–102, 106
accolade, 83
accuracy, 96
achievement, 15, 72
ACID, 6
acknowledgment, 79
acquisition, 41, 55, 58–60, 121
act, 6
adaptability, 6, 7, 24, 30, 49, 52, 60–62, 97
adaptation, 54
address, 2, 5, 12, 16, 17, 23, 25, 33, 35, 36, 58, 59, 66, 73, 89, 92, 94, 95, 97, 101, 102, 107, 108, 115, 120
adherence, 6, 28, 31
adoption, 12, 15, 20, 21, 27, 29, 31, 34, 47, 65, 66, 86, 94, 96, 98, 102
advancement, 35, 42, 81, 102
advent, 25, 45, 50, 64, 105
advocacy, 84, 112
advocate, 63, 115
aftermath, 62
age, 7
agenda, 73
aggression, 19
agility, 59
aim, 71
Alan Turing, 79
algebra, 6, 13, 95
algorithm, 39, 65
alignment, 58
allocation, 87
alternative, 2, 6, 20
ambition, 33, 40, 42
amount, 43
analysis, 2, 27, 39, 44, 49, 65, 89, 91, 94–96, 98, 101, 102
analytic, 95, 97
applicability, 69

application, 19, 27, 28, 63, 71, 98, 113, 117
approach, 3–7, 9, 10, 18, 20, 27, 42, 43, 45, 47, 50, 61, 63, 64, 68, 73, 79, 91, 99–102, 105, 114, 119, 121
architect, 110
architecture, 6, 7, 12, 27, 37, 41, 46, 48, 49, 54, 56–58, 63, 64, 66–69, 74, 87, 90, 95, 99, 101, 105, 107
area, 49, 84
arena, 30
argument, 47
array, 59, 68, 89, 92, 94–97
aspect, 4
assertion, 117
astronomy, 92
attention, 84, 101
audience, 20, 29
audio, 40, 54
availability, 66, 67
average, 96
award, 79, 81–83, 85
awareness, 42, 61
AWS, 66

backing, 18
balance, 26, 63, 68, 71
barrier, 21, 96, 98
base, 56, 58
batch, 69
battle, 20
beacon, 5, 61, 81, 82, 85
beginning, 51, 92
behavior, 38, 39, 65
belief, 4, 5, 119
benefit, 58, 73
birth, 9, 10, 27, 66, 94

bitmap, 44
blend, 75
bottleneck, 48
box, 8
brainchild, 68
brand, 41
bridge, 59, 70, 71
bridging, 73
building, 59
burden, 29
business, 21, 45, 49, 58, 106

cache, 47
caching, 36
capability, 58, 66, 96, 106
capital, 56
career, 2–5, 8, 10, 37, 62, 72, 75, 80, 83, 85, 119
case, 46, 63, 78, 81, 96, 98
Cassandra, 64
catalyst, 70, 80, 83
century, 42
challenge, 2, 5, 7–10, 16, 32, 64, 67, 82, 86, 95, 97–99, 101, 105, 114, 117–119, 121
challenger, 15
change, 34, 41, 61, 66, 72, 80, 91, 96, 118
changer, 66, 67
check, 38
choice, 28, 30, 31, 67, 68, 111
Cisco, 29
citation, 80, 81
city, 110
clarity, 61
class, 76
classification, 39
classroom, 75, 78, 82
clientele, 40

climate, 89, 91, 95, 96
cloud, 25, 29, 51, 64, 66–68, 80, 84, 86, 87, 94, 99, 105
co, 40, 73
code, 24, 31
collaboration, 4, 5, 10, 32, 59, 70, 74, 80, 82, 87
colossus, 116
column, 7, 42–47, 49–52, 113, 115, 120
columnar, 44, 45, 47, 51, 52, 78, 118, 119
combination, 56, 119
commerce, 65
commitment, 5, 7, 61, 62, 66, 75, 83, 87, 114, 119
communication, 59
community, 10, 15, 24, 27, 30–32, 61, 63, 64, 75, 80, 81, 83, 84, 86, 91, 98, 99, 114, 116
company, 44, 53–59, 105
compatibility, 26, 66, 68
competition, 4, 41, 54, 56, 60, 67
competitiveness, 62
competitor, 20
complacency, 116
complex, 2, 4, 6, 7, 9, 22, 23, 25–28, 31, 33, 35–40, 48, 54, 58, 59, 64, 68, 78, 83, 89, 91, 92, 94–96, 102, 103, 105, 112, 115, 117
complexity, 5, 25, 30, 34, 35, 41, 62, 63, 67, 94, 96, 97, 99, 102
compliance, 28
compression, 43, 48, 52, 118, 120
compute, 67, 96
computer, 1–3, 5, 70, 72, 75, 79–84
computing, 25, 27, 51, 64, 66, 79, 81, 83, 86, 94, 95, 105, 117

concept, 1, 9, 12, 22, 23, 36, 37, 39, 40, 47, 78, 99, 114
conceptualization, 36
concern, 31, 99
conclusion, 3, 5, 13, 15, 20, 25, 27, 35, 39, 42, 52, 62, 64, 66, 68, 70, 83, 85, 91, 94, 97, 99, 102, 105, 107, 110, 116, 118, 121
concurrency, 28
conflict, 67
confluence, 8, 35
conformity, 5
confusion, 41
consensus, 65
consistency, 6, 28, 65, 101
consumer, 60
containerization, 87
contemporary, 49, 120
contender, 18, 56
content, 33, 37, 58, 59
context, 100
contrast, 45, 50
contribution, 81
control, 28, 67
convention, 18
core, 5, 11, 20, 23, 25, 47, 50, 53, 64, 90, 94, 95, 99, 103, 108, 119
cornerstone, 12, 23, 31, 64, 71, 110
corporation, 42
cost, 20, 24, 98, 100
counterpart, 47
courage, 119
course, 38
create, 9, 16, 23, 28, 32, 55, 58, 59, 64, 80
creation, 2, 4, 6, 7, 15, 81, 92, 112, 120

creativity, 61, 81, 82
criticism, 31
cube, 39
culmination, 81
culture, 4, 59, 61, 64, 82, 86, 111, 117
curiosity, 1, 3, 5, 8
curve, 34, 62, 96
custom, 28, 38, 112
customer, 18, 22, 34, 42, 56, 58, 60, 62, 65, 105
cutting, 73
cycle, 118

data, 1–16, 21–23, 25, 27–45, 47–55, 57–59, 62–70, 74, 78, 80, 81, 83, 84, 86, 87, 89, 91, 92, 94–103, 105–108, 110–118, 120, 121
database, 1–18, 20–35, 37–47, 49–51, 54–76, 78–81, 83–85, 89, 92, 94–100, 102, 103, 105, 107, 110–119, 121
dataset, 22, 106
deal, 97
decision, 3, 49, 51, 60, 61, 66, 69, 72, 102, 106, 107, 110, 116
decline, 40, 42
decoupling, 67
dedication, 27, 82
degradation, 66
demand, 25, 35, 47, 51, 57, 64, 67, 105
democratization, 32
department, 1
departure, 6, 54
deployment, 87, 97

design, 4, 10, 20, 22, 31, 36, 37, 40, 44, 49, 52, 64, 65, 69, 71, 78, 95, 111, 118
desire, 3, 64, 73, 83
determination, 2, 10
developer, 28
development, 4, 7, 9–12, 14, 15, 17, 22, 24, 26, 27, 29–33, 35–37, 43, 49, 52, 56, 57, 61, 62, 70, 74, 80, 81, 83, 84, 90, 97, 99, 112–114, 117, 119
dictionary, 43
dilution, 41
discipline, 79
discourse, 71, 84, 85
discovery, 39, 97
disparity, 59
disruption, 111, 119
distribution, 30
diversity, 99
divide, 59
document, 103, 105
documentation, 65, 98
domain, 1, 80
dominance, 19
door, 71, 109
down, 6, 74, 86
downfall, 41
downtime, 67
durability, 66
dynamic, 59, 60, 81

e, 65
E.F. Codd, 119
ease, 2, 9, 115
ecosystem, 10, 29, 114, 115
Edgar F. Codd, 114

Edgar F. Codd Innovations Award, 118
edge, 67, 73
education, 29, 37, 72, 98, 99, 118
educator, 75
effectiveness, 19, 24, 93, 101, 104
efficiency, 21, 26, 43, 45, 47, 50, 54, 65, 87, 90, 102
effort, 66, 99, 117
elasticity, 67
element, 4
emergence, 20, 31, 41, 42, 45, 83, 102
emphasis, 4, 10, 12, 22, 35, 49, 64
encapsulation, 38
encoding, 43
encounter, 1, 71, 92, 108
encryption, 67
end, 9, 60
endeavor, 81
engagement, 15, 66
engine, 12
engineering, 3, 114
enrollment, 38
enterprise, 18
entity, 99
entrepreneurship, 60, 62
entry, 21, 34, 72
environment, 4, 22, 59, 71–73, 75, 76, 86, 87, 106, 113, 118
equation, 20, 27, 34, 36, 50, 54, 60, 61, 65, 68, 71, 73, 74, 81, 85–87, 117–119
era, 1, 3, 8, 10, 20, 27, 42, 85, 106, 120
essence, 37, 60, 119
establishment, 99
evolution, 11, 22, 24, 25, 27, 34, 35, 37, 47, 49, 58, 64, 68, 91, 94, 105, 107, 114, 116, 121
example, 2, 26, 31, 36, 39, 44, 60, 92, 94–96, 98, 101, 103, 115
excellence, 9, 20, 23, 61, 66, 83, 119
exception, 4
execution, 9, 12, 14, 22, 26, 29, 73, 98
exercise, 21, 76
expansion, 56, 59
expense, 71
experience, 70, 73–75, 82
experiment, 31
experimentation, 4, 15, 63, 64, 111, 117
exploration, 82, 84, 101, 102, 121
explosion, 33, 92
extensibility, 4, 7, 22–24, 27, 28, 31, 83, 117

face, 65, 104, 121
factor, 7
faculty, 73
failure, 4, 60, 62
fall, 40, 42, 60, 120
fascination, 8
feasibility, 60
feature, 7, 27, 28, 66
federation, 100
feedback, 62, 76, 99
field, 1, 3, 15, 22, 25, 27, 37, 44, 62, 64, 66, 70, 72, 74, 75, 80, 81, 83, 84, 87, 91, 94, 99, 101, 102, 112, 116, 118, 119, 121
finance, 29, 67, 106
fine, 67
flagship, 53
flexibility, 2, 4, 10, 12, 16, 18, 24, 28, 29, 35, 40, 49, 53, 63, 64,

66, 86, 102, 112, 115, 117
fluidity, 6
focus, 21, 61, 66, 73, 75, 84, 96, 102
following, 3, 27, 34, 50, 56, 61, 65, 73, 74, 78, 82, 85–87, 108, 119
footprint, 43
force, 49, 68
forefront, 42, 58
foresight, 42, 60, 86
form, 89
format, 50
forum, 99
foundation, 3, 6, 10, 70, 95, 115, 118
framework, 6, 9, 36, 49, 54, 95, 102, 108, 117
freedom, 4, 29
frequency, 69, 96
friction, 59
friendliness, 96
fruit, 118
functionality, 37
future, 2, 3, 5, 9, 10, 13, 15, 20, 25, 27, 32, 35, 37, 40, 45, 47, 49, 51, 52, 57, 60, 62, 64, 66, 68–70, 75, 80, 81, 84, 85, 87, 94, 97, 99, 101, 105, 107, 108, 110, 112, 114, 116–118, 121

game, 30, 47, 66, 67
gap, 33, 71, 78
generation, 15, 32, 63, 68, 72, 74, 81–83, 87, 114, 116, 118, 121
genius, 61
genomic, 37, 66, 91, 96, 98
goal, 61
government, 20

graph, 105
grid, 92
ground, 64
groundbreaking, 1, 5, 10, 14, 16, 19, 23, 24, 37, 41, 56, 70, 80–82, 85, 94, 97, 110, 112, 120, 121
groundwork, 1, 2, 12, 17, 20, 22, 25, 27, 30, 35, 47, 63, 66, 70, 83, 116
growth, 4, 41, 56, 60, 63, 86
guidance, 59, 72

hallmark, 3
handling, 11, 16, 19, 23, 31, 35, 36, 43, 45, 51, 66, 74, 102, 105, 112, 117
harbinger, 37
hardware, 64
hash, 26
head, 3, 4
health, 37
healthcare, 29, 37, 67, 101
heart, 23, 30, 68, 117
high, 20, 29, 55, 66, 69, 92, 97
history, 23, 24, 56
honor, 79
horizon, 85
humidity, 89
hurdle, 59
hybrid, 22, 49, 68

idea, 30, 64
identification, 31
image, 92
impact, 2, 5, 15, 17, 21, 22, 27, 32, 35, 37, 45, 49, 60, 65, 67, 69, 79, 81, 83–85, 91, 110, 114, 118, 119

Index 129

impetus, 80
implementation, 49
importance, 42, 49, 59–62, 70, 72, 73, 76, 80, 82–84, 86, 107
improvement, 27, 99, 111
in, 1–13, 15–45, 47–52, 54–76, 78, 80–87, 89–92, 94–97, 99–108, 111–121
inability, 57
inception, 5, 60
inconsistency, 2
incorporation, 21, 59
increase, 63
independence, 12
indexing, 25, 29, 36, 44
individual, 81, 83, 118
industry, 2, 4, 8, 10, 15, 17, 18, 20, 23, 26, 31, 32, 34, 37, 40, 41, 49, 57–60, 62, 65, 66, 68–70, 72, 74, 75, 82, 84, 85, 110–112, 114–116, 119, 121
inefficiency, 12, 48
inertia, 94
inevitability, 60, 62
infancy, 1, 8, 101
inflexibility, 1
influence, 12, 22, 25, 37, 40, 47, 49, 63, 69, 70, 72, 75, 79, 82, 84, 85, 112, 114, 117, 118, 121
information, 1, 28, 29, 37, 64, 103, 120
infrastructure, 25, 29, 41, 64
Ingres, 2–4, 6–9, 11–23, 25, 26, 60, 61, 73, 115, 117, 119
Ingres, 6, 119
initiative, 62, 74

innovation, 4, 6–10, 14, 17, 18, 20, 22, 23, 26, 31–33, 35, 37, 40, 42, 54, 59–61, 64, 68, 70, 75, 80–86, 110–112, 114, 116–121
inquiry, 10, 82, 116, 121
insight, 6, 43, 117
inspiration, 5
instance, 1, 4, 14, 19, 22, 28, 31, 38, 60, 64, 65, 67, 69, 70, 78, 84, 86, 91, 96, 98, 104, 105, 112, 114, 119, 120
institution, 98
integration, 12, 36, 39, 41, 54, 57–59, 63, 80, 84, 94, 98–100, 105, 107
integrity, 1, 2, 4, 6, 16, 28, 65, 78, 100, 101
intellect, 8
intelligence, 45, 49, 51, 59, 80, 94, 105
interaction, 12, 105, 117
interest, 19, 71
interface, 53, 99, 101
internet, 33, 57, 63
interoperability, 12, 96, 99, 102
introduction, 7, 9, 12, 14, 21, 23, 25, 27, 37, 47, 49, 57, 63, 91, 113, 115, 117
invention, 89, 91
isolation, 4
issue, 48
iteration, 63

join, 2, 26, 103
journey, 1, 3–5, 7, 8, 18, 23, 35–37, 40, 42, 57, 59, 60, 62, 65, 66, 69, 70, 72, 81, 97, 114, 118, 120, 121

key, 4–6, 9, 13, 17, 18, 35, 43, 45, 49, 60, 66, 73, 83, 85, 92, 99, 100, 103, 105, 115, 117
kind, 92
knowledge, 3, 15, 37, 39, 70, 71, 73, 83, 96, 118

lack, 31, 54
landmark, 15
landscape, 2, 7, 8, 12, 15, 18, 20, 25, 27, 30, 33, 35, 37, 39, 41, 42, 45, 47, 49, 51, 55–60, 62, 68, 70, 79, 83, 85, 89, 92, 97, 99, 102, 110–112, 114, 116, 117, 119, 121
language, 12, 15, 21, 23, 38, 94, 96, 103
latency, 66–68, 71, 89, 100, 101
leader, 25, 41, 58, 59
leadership, 58, 59
leap, 26, 97, 107
learning, 51, 59, 62, 66, 75, 76, 80, 84, 94, 96, 102, 105, 120
lecturer, 71
legacy, 5, 10, 13, 15, 18, 23, 25, 30, 32, 35, 37, 40, 49, 51, 52, 57, 60, 64, 66, 68, 70, 75, 81, 84, 85, 91, 94, 107, 111, 112, 114, 116–119, 121
length, 43
lens, 95
lesson, 60
level, 18
leverage, 12, 25, 31, 47, 52, 58, 59, 63, 64, 67, 70, 87, 96, 99, 102, 105
license, 30
licensing, 24, 29, 31
life, 10
lifetime, 81
light, 40, 87, 121
line, 41, 58, 59
locality, 50
lock, 31, 68
loss, 2
luminary, 3
luster, 57

machine, 51, 59, 66, 80, 84, 94, 96, 102, 105, 120
maintenance, 69
making, 2, 9, 18, 24, 28–31, 37, 49, 51, 60, 61, 67, 69, 95, 98, 102, 106, 107, 110, 116
management, 1–3, 5, 7–10, 13, 15, 20–23, 25, 27, 28, 31, 33–35, 37, 40–42, 45, 47, 49, 51, 52, 58, 59, 62, 64, 66–70, 74, 78, 80, 81, 83, 84, 87, 89, 94–99, 102, 105, 107, 110, 112, 114, 118, 120
manipulation, 6, 9, 38, 95
manner, 37, 47, 105
mapping, 100
mark, 8, 27, 49, 75, 83, 112, 117, 118, 121
marker, 83
market, 18–20, 29, 33–35, 41, 42, 54, 56, 57, 59–62, 67, 69
marketing, 18, 19, 34, 39, 54, 65
marketplace, 121
master, 110
material, 74
mean, 94
media, 105
medicine, 66

memory, 45
mentor, 71, 74, 114
mentorship, 74, 75, 82, 118
method, 39
Michael Stonebraker, 5, 10, 13, 15, 22–24, 30, 33, 35, 36, 40, 42, 60, 62, 64, 66, 68, 70, 72, 91, 92, 94, 116, 119, 121
Michael Stonebraker's, 1, 3, 5, 8, 15, 18, 25, 27, 30, 32, 37, 49, 52, 57, 58, 62, 64, 66, 75, 80, 83, 85, 87, 89, 107, 110, 112, 114, 116, 118, 121
milestone, 31, 49, 80
mind, 9, 23, 66, 90
mindset, 15
minicomputer, 18
mining, 39
mission, 28
mix, 19
model, 1–3, 6, 9, 12, 15, 22, 23, 25, 28, 29, 31, 36, 38–40, 48, 51, 52, 89, 97, 101, 102, 105, 112–114, 117–119
modeling, 66, 89, 91, 95, 113
modification, 30
modularity, 69
moment, 11, 20, 24, 26, 47, 58, 59, 64, 75, 91, 94
Mondrian, 7, 8, 42, 45, 47–49, 115, 118
move, 37, 41, 58, 70, 73
movement, 13, 27, 30–32, 103
multi, 52, 68, 91, 92, 102, 105
multimedia, 7, 33, 35–37, 58, 59
myriad, 105

name, 38
narrative, 19, 114
nature, 4, 21, 24, 42, 59, 60, 74, 80, 95, 106, 110
necessity, 62
need, 2, 9, 11, 25, 36, 39, 43, 48, 49, 53, 57, 64, 66, 67, 69, 70, 80, 83, 86, 92, 95, 96, 98, 100, 115
network, 1, 2, 9, 11, 65, 67, 100, 114
niche, 35
node, 1, 65
norm, 96
normalization, 6, 76, 78
notion, 23, 81
number, 102

object, 7, 23, 25, 31, 34–39, 41, 57, 81, 113, 115, 117, 119
obstacle, 98
offering, 28, 47, 67
office, 71
on, 3, 4, 7–10, 12, 14, 15, 17, 18, 20–22, 27, 29–32, 35, 37, 39, 40, 44, 45, 47, 49, 51, 55, 57, 61, 64–67, 69, 72–75, 78–81, 83–86, 89, 91, 92, 95, 96, 98, 99, 102, 108, 110, 112–114, 117–121
one, 6, 16, 20, 22, 24, 33, 35, 71, 81, 98, 119
openness, 22
opportunity, 58, 68
optimization, 6, 9, 12, 14, 21, 22, 64, 73, 78, 98, 100, 102, 108
optimizer, 2, 14, 22
option, 2, 29
organization, 1

origin, 99
other, 21, 22, 29, 37, 59, 67, 71, 96
overhead, 25, 89, 94, 101, 103
ownership, 57

pace, 57, 62
paradigm, 17, 37, 42, 65, 87, 95, 114–116
parent, 1
partitioning, 29
partnership, 41
passion, 2
path, 4, 5, 12, 63, 118
peak, 66
peer, 76, 85
penchant, 3
penetration, 41
performance, 2, 4, 6, 7, 9, 12, 14, 18, 20–22, 24, 26, 29, 30, 36, 43, 44, 46–53, 55, 59, 63, 64, 66–68, 79, 84, 95, 97, 99–102, 113, 115, 118, 120
period, 41, 56
perseverance, 35
persistence, 63, 64
perspective, 80
philosopher, 118
philosophy, 5, 9, 23, 29, 53, 117, 119
pioneer, 30, 60, 75, 79, 91, 92, 94, 119–121
plan, 14
plateau, 56
platform, 15, 73, 98, 99
player, 20, 30, 37
plethora, 84
point, 20, 64, 89
polyglot, 63, 64

Polystore, 99, 101, 102, 105–110, 121
pond, 117
popularity, 31
position, 25, 29, 47, 70
Postgres, 27
potential, 2, 9, 20, 30, 37, 41, 84, 86, 97, 98, 100–102, 105, 107, 110
power, 5, 8, 18, 23, 25, 32, 60, 94, 101, 103, 105, 114, 116, 121
practice, 73, 74, 78
precedence, 20
precedent, 69
precipitation, 96
predecessor, 23, 25
presence, 18
pressure, 20, 89, 96
price, 57
principle, 9, 62, 64
problem, 1, 4, 59
process, 51, 58, 69, 78, 97, 98, 106, 120
processing, 6, 26, 36, 45, 47, 49, 65, 68–70, 73, 94, 97, 98, 105, 106
processor, 26
product, 36, 41, 43, 53, 57–59, 61, 62
professor, 71, 74, 114
profile, 20
program, 2
programming, 23, 94, 98
progress, 18, 64, 114
project, 23, 24, 27, 31, 42, 59, 62, 68–70, 74, 86, 98
proliferation, 111
promise, 108

Index 133

proposition, 41
prowess, 94
public, 24, 56
purpose, 61
pursuit, 3, 9, 17, 20, 23, 33, 35, 42, 66, 83, 85, 111, 112, 119

query, 2, 6, 7, 9, 12, 14, 21–24, 26, 29, 36–39, 43–47, 73, 78, 94–103, 105, 108, 111, 113, 115, 118, 120
querying, 13, 21, 35, 86, 96, 101, 117
quest, 9, 37, 99, 121
quo, 2, 3, 6, 9, 13, 15, 20, 27, 30, 35, 64, 80, 112, 114, 116, 117, 119

range, 24, 28, 31, 93, 107, 111
rate, 64, 107
ratio, 48
reach, 61, 68, 94
read, 7, 43, 45, 50, 79, 113, 115
reality, 36, 37
realization, 36
realm, 1, 5, 8, 27, 30, 35, 42, 47, 62, 64–66, 68, 80, 89, 105, 114, 116
rebellion, 3, 5–8, 10, 116
receipt, 79, 83
reception, 40
recipient, 79
recognition, 20, 72, 80, 82–84
record, 50
redundancy, 1, 78
reflection, 79
region, 96
regression, 39
relation, 35

relationship, 68, 74
release, 15, 24, 26, 56
relevance, 30, 47, 52, 62, 81, 91
reliability, 18, 28, 29, 84
reluctance, 41, 98
reminder, 18, 42, 64, 83, 84, 121
reorganization, 2
replication, 65, 100
representation, 95, 97, 108
reputation, 20, 58
research, 15, 19–21, 31, 33, 37, 44, 56, 66, 70, 73, 74, 80, 83–85, 89, 92, 97–100, 109, 110, 117, 118
resilience, 4, 60, 68, 97, 114
resistance, 34, 63, 65, 94
resolution, 67
resource, 69, 87
response, 14, 20, 23, 33, 48, 60, 62, 86, 99, 115, 120
responsiveness, 36
rest, 67
restructuring, 41, 57
result, 24, 41, 82
rethinking, 6, 34
retrieval, 6, 7, 9, 38, 42, 43, 45, 47–49, 51, 64, 65, 102, 113, 118, 120
return, 70
revolution, 13, 27, 30
rewriting, 7
ride, 57
right, 60
rigidity, 18
rigor, 75, 81
rise, 25, 29, 31, 33, 35, 40–42, 49, 52, 60, 68, 80, 86, 120
risk, 65, 121
road, 4, 5

robustness, 28, 29, 31
role, 15, 27, 29, 45, 49, 70, 74, 79, 81, 83, 97, 114, 119
rollercoaster, 57
row, 43, 45–47, 49, 50, 78, 113
rule, 7, 26
run, 43

s, 1–10, 15–18, 20–22, 25, 27–32, 34–37, 39, 41, 42, 47–49, 51–53, 56–62, 64–66, 68–70, 73, 75, 79–87, 89, 91, 94, 96, 98, 99, 107, 110–121
saga, 35
scalability, 9, 10, 29, 36, 49, 52, 64, 66, 69, 70, 84–86, 90, 95, 97, 113, 115
scale, 29, 45, 48, 67, 70, 74, 86, 89, 95, 105
scaling, 54, 64
scan, 22
scenario, 28, 38, 44
schema, 12, 76, 100, 101
schemas, 64
science, 1–3, 5, 70, 72, 75, 79–84, 91, 96, 107, 114
search, 25
section, 5, 15, 30, 35, 40, 42, 45, 47, 66, 83, 97, 105, 107, 114, 117, 119
sector, 42, 59, 69
security, 31, 67, 101
selling, 41
sense, 3, 61, 99
sentiment, 105, 119
separation, 69
series, 3, 17, 29, 55–58, 60, 68, 78, 97, 119, 121

serve, 62, 70, 87, 118, 121
serverless, 105
service, 31
set, 2, 8, 13–15, 21, 23, 26, 27, 37, 40, 41, 59, 81
setting, 9, 20, 69, 84
share, 20, 67, 73, 98, 99
shift, 2, 12, 19, 25, 33, 42, 45, 49, 50, 72, 75, 84, 95, 102, 113, 114, 116
shopping, 66
significance, 27, 29, 30, 37, 61, 62, 82, 84, 111, 117
simplicity, 94
size, 48, 100
skepticism, 19, 34, 65
skyline, 110
software, 10, 29, 30, 56, 84
solution, 48, 58, 59, 64, 86, 94, 99, 111
solving, 4, 59
source, 10, 13, 22, 24, 27, 29–32, 61, 84–87, 100, 101, 112–114
speaker, 82
speech, 80
speed, 9, 12, 24
spirit, 4, 5, 8, 10, 13, 15, 22, 24, 30, 32, 35, 37, 40, 42, 57, 64, 70, 83, 87, 112, 114, 116, 118–121
spotlight, 25
staff, 34
stage, 2, 8, 9, 13, 15, 20, 21, 40, 81
standard, 12, 15, 21, 23, 28, 36–38, 59, 67, 117
standpoint, 59
startup, 55, 57, 59
state, 65, 68
statement, 62

Index 135

status, 2, 3, 6, 9, 13, 15, 20, 27, 30, 35, 38, 64, 80, 112, 114, 116, 117, 119
step, 66
stock, 57
stone, 60, 116
Stonebraker, 78
storage, 7, 9, 12, 14, 38, 42, 43, 45, 47–49, 51, 52, 64, 67, 78, 80, 96, 99, 102, 105, 108, 115, 118–120
store, 7, 37, 38, 43, 45–47, 49, 50, 66, 103, 105, 117, 120
story, 33, 35, 57
strategy, 98
stream, 68
streaming, 69, 106
structure, 1, 2, 16, 76, 97
struggle, 20, 22, 95, 99, 105
study, 46, 84, 96
subset, 47
success, 2, 4, 5, 7, 12, 16, 20, 41, 54, 56, 60, 61, 63, 68, 104, 120
suite, 57
summary, 22, 30, 37, 49, 112, 114
support, 4, 7, 22, 23, 25, 27, 28, 31, 35, 83, 99, 107, 111, 112, 115
sustainability, 31
synergy, 58, 74
syntax, 103
system, 4, 7, 12–15, 22, 23, 25–27, 31, 33–37, 39–41, 55, 58, 63–67, 69, 74, 85, 92, 97–99, 103, 105, 108, 111

table, 22, 43
takeaway, 60
tale, 57, 66, 114
talent, 61, 75
tapestry, 5, 60
teaching, 75
team, 2, 4, 12–15, 18, 20, 23, 24, 26, 27, 33, 35, 36, 42, 58, 59, 61–65, 68, 70, 90, 91, 98, 99
teamwork, 61, 82
tech, 55, 58, 64, 72
technology, 2, 5, 8–10, 13, 15, 18, 20, 23, 27, 30, 32, 33, 35, 37, 40–42, 49, 57–64, 66, 68, 70, 71, 75, 80, 81, 83–85, 87, 89, 99, 107, 109, 112, 114, 116, 121
telecommunications, 106
temperature, 89, 92, 94, 96
tenacity, 83
tenure, 1
term, 41
testament, 5, 8, 13, 18, 23, 24, 32, 35, 57, 59, 72, 83, 114, 121
testing, 63
text, 25, 33
theme, 34
theory, 6, 73, 78
thinking, 79
throughput, 20, 68, 71
time, 1, 2, 9, 14, 20, 23, 29, 39, 40, 44, 51, 53, 56, 58, 65, 66, 89, 92, 94, 96, 97, 100, 106, 107, 111
title, 119
today, 22, 40, 57, 64, 81, 84, 112
tool, 37, 91, 95
traction, 18, 19, 24, 34, 97
trade, 71
trading, 69
tradition, 15

trajectory, 3, 87, 116
transaction, 28, 29, 58, 66
transfer, 70, 118
transformation, 42, 57, 103
transit, 67
transition, 31, 34, 43, 58, 60, 65, 66, 72, 98
transparency, 10, 31
tree, 1
trend, 49
triumph, 66, 67
trophy, 81
troubleshooting, 31
turning, 20, 64, 89
tutelage, 72
type, 23, 28

underpinning, 13
understanding, 9, 37, 58, 60, 62, 78, 91
undertaking, 62
university, 1, 38
up, 1, 2, 43, 59, 67, 86, 105
update, 101
usability, 26, 28, 113
usage, 40
use, 2, 6, 9, 30, 31, 81, 99, 105, 115
user, 9, 10, 20, 25, 28, 35, 53, 65, 96, 98, 99, 103, 117
utility, 66
utilization, 47

value, 62
variety, 28, 53
velocity, 68
vendor, 31, 68
venture, 60, 64
versatility, 29, 52, 93, 104, 105, 109, 111

version, 12
viability, 4, 15
video, 40, 54
view, 106
vision, 9, 10, 15, 16, 20, 24, 25, 27, 35, 41, 55, 61, 62, 81–83, 91, 92
visionary, 9, 10, 13, 30, 58, 59
volatility, 57
volume, 30, 68, 94, 95
volunteer, 31

war, 8
warehousing, 31, 45, 51, 68, 115
Watson, 101
wave, 49, 84
way, 2, 3, 9, 10, 13, 15, 22, 26, 27, 35, 40, 42, 45, 48, 50–52, 57, 59, 62, 84, 85, 91, 94, 97, 99, 100, 102, 107, 110, 112, 114, 117, 120
wealth, 30, 62
web, 31, 57
whole, 59
willingness, 3, 4, 8, 9, 18, 61, 64, 66, 117–119, 121
wisdom, 3, 9, 37, 117, 119
work, 1, 4, 9, 10, 15–17, 22, 30, 36, 42, 49, 61, 70, 80–84, 95, 96, 110–117, 120
workload, 7
world, 3, 5, 8, 15, 18, 19, 23, 27, 30, 35, 37, 49, 52, 58, 59, 62, 64, 66, 70, 72, 74, 81, 98, 101, 119–121

year, 96

Milton Keynes UK
Ingram Content Group UK Ltd.
UKHW020318021124
450424UK00013B/1325